ISLAM AND GOD-CENTRICITY: REASSESSING FUNDAMENTAL THEOLOGICAL ASSUMPTIONS

by

Shaykh Arif Abdul Hussain

© Shaykh Arif Abdul Hussain 2019

All rights reserved. No part of this book may be reproduced, stored, or transmitted in any form or by any means, electronic or otherwise, including photocopying, recording, Internet, or any storage and retrieval system without prior written permission from the copyright owner.

Printed in the United Kingdom.

ISBN 978-1-9998621-2-1

Published by:
Sajjadiyya Press
60 Weoley Park Road
Selly Oak
Birmingham, B29 6RB

Author: Shaykh Arif Abdul Hussain

CONTENTS

ACKNOWLEDGEMENTS V

FORWARD VII

NIGHT ONE 1

NIGHT TWO 16

NIGHT THREE 29

NIGHT FOUR 43

NIGHT FIVE 58

NIGHT SIX 75

NIGHT SEVEN 92

NIGHT EIGHT 107

NIGHT NINE 121

NIGHT TEN 137

ACKNOWLEDGEMENTS

The following lectures were delivered at IUS in Manchester (UK) on the first ten nights of Muharram 1438 (October 2016). The author wishes to express his sincere gratitude to the community for their appreciation of these lectures. The author also wishes to thank Ms Samar Mashadi, Dr Wahid Amin, Riaz Jessa and his dear daughter Mahdiyah Abdul Hussain for their efforts in the editing and publication process of this series.

FOREWORD:

In the name of God, the All-beneficent, the All-merciful;
All praise belongs to God.
May benedictions and peace be upon Muḥammad,
His apostle and the best of His creation,
And upon the Pure Ones of his family.

THIS BOOK IS THE SECOND VOLUME in the *Islam and God-Centricity* series. It is comprised of the edited transcripts of lectures delivered by Shaykh Arif Abdul Hussain in Muharram 1438 (October 2016). In accordance with its subtitle, *Reassessing Fundamental Theological Assumptions*, the lectures in this book aim at reviving a pivotal feature of Prophet Muḥammad's message that was intended to be practiced by each of his adherents in every generation: the attitude of sincere inquiry and continual learning. This includes the questioning of fundamental theological assumptions of the religion (*dīn*) prevailing in the culture that one is born into. The importance of this facet of the Prophet's message cannot be overstated. Indeed, the plethora of challenges faced by Muslims today, such as sectarianism, terrorism, Islamophobia, and identity crisis, is a direct consequence of overlooking this fundamental aspect of religion. Moreover, it is a prerequisite to authentic spirituality, as well as part of the constitution of the God-centred human being.

Accordingly, the themes in this book include: God, purpose, and the meaning of life; eschatology in terms of humanity on earth, and the human soul in the Hereafter; the meaning of *ʿamal al-ṣāliḥ*; assumptions about the Quran and its interpretation; assumptions about the Prophet Muḥammad and the Imams; and a range of other theological issues.

The questioning of one's core assumptions and long-held beliefs can be a painful process, but perseverance will lead to catharsis and growth towards Allah (SWT) *inshāllah*. This work is not intended to cause offence. It is done with the intention of reviving the spirit of inquiry that is the essential hallmark of what it is to be human, and by priority, of religion (*dīn*) too.

The editor takes full responsibility for any errors in the text. If there are any questions, comments, or constructive criticisms, please forward them to Al-Mahdi Institute.

Night One

We thank Allah for the opportunity to once again witness the month of Muharram and for allowing us to show our love and affection to our blessed Imam Husayn. We also thank Allah for letting us make use of this platform in order to gain further insight into His good pleasure and to share goodness with each other.

As a prelude to our topic and discussions for this year, I begin by stating that we come into this world with a belief of fulfilling a purpose and a sense of wanting to become something. This world is seen as a place of opportunity for us to get somewhere. There is a calling deep within our own human state that there is some purpose; some profound purpose for which we are here in this world. There has to be something that intimately appeals to us and there is something specific to be achieved. When we analyse and think about it carefully, we realise that our place of birth, time of birth, parents, cultures and religions that define us and give a sense of life seem to be secondary – almost arbitrary. Our statuses and our genders do not appear to have that much importance. That "purpose" seems to be much more intimate than whatever else we are born into and whatever they dictate to us about the meaning of life. Intuitively, we have this realisation that we are on this earth to play a definite and a substantive role.

Taking birth in a culture, religion, family, location, and timeframe are factors that condition and shape us. They influence our understanding of what life is all about. They influence how we perceive our purpose, shape our worldview and inform our sense of existence. This can be very limiting and restrictive. For example, if our religious world view is that we are merely here on this earth to pray, fast, perform Hajj, die and go on to the next stage of life, then of course there will not be an impetus within us to seek, search, and explore the secrets of the heavens and the earth.

We would not have that want – that yearning – to delve deep into the seas and uncover its secrets! We would not have the want to explore the heavens and to master them because our whole sense of purpose is determined by this very simplistic belief that we are created to fast, pray, perform Hajj, and then return to the Creator. This is an unexplored sense of existence that the cradle of culture and naïve religious understanding has instilled within us. We have not attained and achieved it after contemplation and exploration with an open mind. We have been conditioned to this way of thinking, and as such, this sense of purpose does not satisfy our need to have a meaningful life.

The Quran, in order to move us from such assumptions, invites us to think accurately, to reflect and to ponder. Allah says, "And it is He who has spread the earth wide and placed on it firm mountains and running waters and created two sexes of every plant; and it is He who causes the night to cover the day. Verily, in all this there are messages for people who think" (13:3) These verses, and many others, are asking people to step back from their conditioning and upbringing and instead to introspect – to look deep within themselves and try and understand what is going on for themselves. The Quran states, "Do you presume that We have created you in vain and that you shall not be returned to us?" (23:115). Is this *your* assumption?

My assumption is that I was born into a religion and God has favoured me, and that is why I will be the one who is saved. I have never been critical enough to ask, but what about my neighbour who has taken birth in another religion? To the best of my recollection I did not choose the religion of my birth and my neighbour also did not choose his religion, so why would God favour me and not him? This in itself requires us to ponder, reflect and conclude that, no actually, the religion of birth is quite arbitrary compared to the "real" thing.

Another thing that we need to ask ourselves is that until and unless we are instilled with a "real" sense of purpose, are we *really* living a life or is it a life that is being lived in a half state? Think about what Imam Sadiq said. "A person who arrives into religion with the people, leaves the religion with the people. A person who arrives into the religion through their own deliberation stays firm within their religion even when the mountains tremble and shake." Therefore, if I am born into this religion and I lead my life in accordance with the teachings of this religion that are often influenced by my culture, time, and location, then obviously I am not invested in the message. I was born into this message just like my neighbour who was born into a slightly different message. We are both invested in our own messages in a half manner; we are in essence semi-invested. But what if I were to understand for myself, and I were to seek and arrive at the knowledge of the truth of the message? Imagine my level of investment and commitment to the message! I would then live a full and substantive life. A life that is not a wasteful life.

The Quran states, "The life of this world is nothing but a passing delight, and the life in the Hereafter is by far better for all who are conscious of God. Will you not then use your reason?"(6:32) This life of ours is being described as a momentary form of pleasure, a pass time. It is actually describing this state of ours as one in which we are not fully invested. It is describing a state where we are not fully living life but merely existing, and that too in a half-hearted manner – an arbitrary life. What then is "real" life? A "real" life is where we are fully committed to the purpose of our creation. What brings about that full commitment is an accurate understanding of what is happening – of what life is all about. So the Quran says: "Do they not think?" "Do they not understand?" "Do they not reflect?" "In there are signs for the people of the heart." "In there are signs for those who reflect." "In there are signs for those who are mindful." "In there are signs for those who are conscious." Allah is awakening us to the inner feeling within us that surely there is more to this.

Are you really living a life, or are you on precarious grounds? Are you sure?

The fact that I can be so dismayed and can entertain the question whether I am sure about my purpose, shows that I am not truly grounded in it. I am not grounded in the purpose because I have not arrived at it through a process of investigation and contemplation. It has been given to me. Had it come from me, it would have been very different. Let me give an example: imagine that we are trapped inside a room with a group of people. The room has an exit door but there is a common belief that there is a lion outside the door. So the belief that there is a lion outside the door is known to us, but it will not stop us from going near the door or peeking out in order to escape. However, if we *knew* that there was indeed a lion outside the door, our state would be very different. We would be extremely cautious of the door. That is the difference between when we take birth into a belief system and when we arrive at a concrete understanding of the nature of our own existence by ourselves.

Similarly, the Quran implies that why are they not critical of whatever belief systems they follow? Can God ordain anything that is unchaste, which is indecent? He says to the Meccans, you believe that I have ordained such and such. Can God ever ordain anything that is indecent? God does not ordain that which is indecent and that which is reprehensible. So, I say, why aren't you critical? It is your God-given right to be critical; that is how you ought to be. You should not be taking anything at face value. There should not be any assumptions without critique. So what if our forefathers did whatever they did? What if they were wrong? "But when they are told to follow what God has revealed, some answer, 'Nay, we shall follow only that which we found our forefathers believing in and doing.' Why, even if their forefathers did not use their reason at all, and were devoid of all guidance?" (2:170)

I ask a simple question: What if we just follow culture, family traditions, and whatever we are told, but they are wrong? What then? Then where do we stand? That question was enough to startle the Meccans and to awaken them. What if your forefathers were wrong, then what excuse will you present? Just because they have been going down that route, does that mean that it is the correct way to reach to the destination? What if they were all misled? What if it wasted a lot of time? Would you want to do that? It is such a logical proposition; what if they were wrong? At least when you ascertain that they were right you have full stake holding. If you investigate it critically and they happen to be wrong, then you would be led aright. The Quran often points at this state of humankind – that you are not thinking. You are not critical. You have taken birth into these systems. You have assumed many things and have never checked these assumptions.

The present community may be thinking, but that was for the Meccans; we are not the Meccans; we are born Muslims. But look at the Sunni and Shia– the fact that they can curse each other. The fact that they are killing each other throughout the world. Does this not in itself show that neither of them are thinking? They have taken birth into their own systems and they have taken it as God's truth. They have committed themselves to it but neither of them are sure within themselves – unless, of course, they are very arrogant about it and they are leading their lives accordingly. What if I was to ask that how much of our history do we know to be accurate? How much of our theology do we know to be accurate? How many of our assumptions do we know to be accurate?

If I were to ask a Christian that question, he would put his hands up and say, "I don't know". A Muslim would say "I don't know", a Hindu "I don't know", a Buddhist "I don't know" and similarly the Shia, the Sunni, the Wahhabi, the Salafi, the Barelvi, the Deobandi will all say, "I don't actually know". Mankind is still in the same position it has always been. The Quran was not addressing the Meccans with the particularity of them being Meccans in that time and place. It was addressing Meccans as human beings because it is a trait of humanity that we all possess. We take birth and lazily go about our lives, living them uncritically.

The fact that we are not ready to go into the hereafter shows that we have not found God. The fact that I panic at the point of death and the fact that when the crushing pain comes on my chest, I stretch out my hand for a physician and make deals with God, "O Lord, I will pray a hundred units of prayer. I will pay a thousand pounds, ten thousand pounds, will offer one sacrificial animal (*qurbāni*), ten sacrificial animals!" The fact that I become so bewildered. I become so confused and perplexed. The fact that I lose my composure at that point. The fact that when I am sailing in the stormy waters and the storm grips me with fear, I lose all sense of protocol and I cry out to Allah and lose sense of my dignity and calm. All this shows that there is no surety of the Hereafter! It is one thing for me to claim I know where I am going and I am sure of it. It is another thing being invested in that belief with certitude. The fact that I am not sure of myself when I go into the Hereafter – of what will happen to me on the first night – shows that I have not found my God at all! What purpose have I served? For which purpose have I lived? What life have I lived and what is the objective that I have attained if this is my situation?

The fact that I find it difficult at times to dig into my pocket and give in the way of God shows that saying is one thing and really knowing it and being invested in it is another thing. Of course, if a person really and truly believed that the verse of the Quran that if you give in the way of God, God will multiply it seventy times over, is true, then they will not hesitate in giving would they? Surely, if a person were to digest the verse that Allah gives life, takes life, and no soul dies without the consent of God, then such a soul would rid itself of fear or would be able to overcome fear even if it cannot rid itself of fear. "And no human being can die save by God's leave, at a pre-ordained time."(3:145) Such a soul would not feel insecurity.

If a person had digested the verses that God gives dignity and respect, that He prescribes humility as a means to reach God Himself and that He gives victory and defeat – both of them are from God in order for him to attain a greater level of existence. If a soul knew all this, it would not be concerned about what people say and it would not be concerned about winning the battle. It would be more concerned about becoming a greater human being, more secure, upright, righteous, and truthful. It would not fear people or be filled with anxieties and apprehensions, or have given itself over to superstitions. Mere proclamation of all this is one thing but being absolutely invested in these truths is another. The Quran says, "Do they not think?" Why don't we check our assumptions critically in order to arrive at an understanding that can sustain a worthy life? If we do this, it gives true birth to a real individual.

Let us honestly accept that we are all very insecure. God is only significant because belief in Him gives us security. We are so frightened, and therefore, we believe that God will save us – of course He will, there is no doubt, but the way Husayn loved God was very different to the way I love God. On the day of Ashura amidst the naked blades that were cutting him into pieces, he supplicated, "O Lord! You are the one I rely upon in every state. There is none worthy of worship other than You." This is Husayn. The level to which he is invested in that purpose is very different to the level to which even his own companions were invested. Husayn's God, Husayn's love and devotion, Husayn's commitment, is very different to mine. Until and unless I awaken, I may never arrive at that level of existence, at that sense of righteousness, at that sense of purpose.

Observe the world we live in. It is a sick and an ailing world. Imagine an amazing world in which seven billion people acknowledge that we have common values, human values. We are one and the same at the core of our humanity. Essentially, we are the same. We all value the worth of human life. We all agree that poverty is a sickness, injustice cannot be tolerated, there should not be any distinction by way of gender, colour, religion, age or status. We all say there ought to be harmonious coexistence. We all believe in common human values. Yet look at these seven billion people who are at each other's throats all the time. It is a crazy world, a sick world in which people know the truth and are distanced from the truth. Show me one place in this world where we do not have strife; where division, battle, war, crime, injustices are not rife? And show me one place in the world where people are not mature enough to understand that there are common human values; that truthfulness is good, that justice is good, charity is good, giving life is good, respecting the other is good? Everybody agrees and yet they are out to finish each other off. Bring me one group of people that do not point the finger at the other one and say, "We are better than you." Everyone does the same thing, "I am better than you."

Sadi, the celebrated Persian poet of the medieval period, in his book "Gulistan", narrated that a father took his child to the mosque. They walked inside an old mosque where people used to sleep in the forecourt and grounds. He took him at the time of night prayer before the morning prayers. The child in amazement said, "Father they are asleep." The father replied, "It would have been better had you been asleep on this night. This statement of arrogance of yours shows that I have made a mistake by bringing you so early to the mosque." This piety and godliness has led to ungodliness. Which one of us does not point the finger at the other and say, "I am so righteous. I am better than you." We all have this sickness.

Look at humanity today. Look at the state of humanity. It is a sickening state, a pitiful state. Take a look at the television. Look at how people are dying, how children are dying, how they are hungry, how they are being butchered, and how they are being slaughtered. And this is happening in the 21st century! How can this be possible in the 21st century? You can imagine these things happening in the barbaric Arabia to which the Prophet was sent. But this is happening in the 21st century and I am calm. I sleep peacefully. It does not affect me. I have become de-sensitised. Truly, it is a sick world in which we live but the problem is not that the world is sick. The problem is that *we are sick*. We are very mistaken in stating that the world is sick. No, I am the sick one that makes the world sick. Had I been caring for the plight of the orphans and of others, I would be paining. I would not be sitting here talking about the world being sick. I would be addressing my own sickness.

So, we all understand these beautiful human values and yet the world does not abide by them. We have the greatest level of intellectual appreciation of goodness and the least commitment to it. It is amazing. We all know what is right but seven billion people cannot stop this world dragging itself to its own destruction. What brings this level of complacency in our minds is that we are not invested in a sense of purpose. We need to understand this core issue that we will discuss in the lectures to follow: the success and salvation of humanity at large guarantees my success. Until now, my assumption has been that I can be righteous within myself and the rest of humanity can go wherever it goes. This assumption needs to be checked. We have to understand that if I am on a ship and others on the ship are making holes, then I am going to drown with them. When we learn that this is a common abode for us all, that is when we will all be led to our success and salvation. We all need to awaken to a deep sense of purpose.

What has really contributed to us not awakening is our laziness in critically looking at our assumptions, our history, and our theology. I repeat: you and I are born into a packaged religion. Taking birth inside a packaged religion, we will never challenge it; we will never question it. In fact, there are things in our religious practices that are inconsistent with our human condition but religion will justify them for us, causing us to become inconsistent with our better judgment of how things ought to be. Therefore, religions and cultures contribute to complacency in the minds of its followers if they lazily assume everything to be accurate without making the effort to think critically about things that are inconsistent with the natural human state that the Quran is ordaining.

I salute the ancestors of the people from the subcontinent as I salute the grandfathers of the Arabs as the Persians to whom Islam came for the first time. I salute them because they were free individuals. When the Prophet delivered his message, they listened with open minds. They were able to break their assumptions – their idols – and through that they were led aright. Imagine if somebody comes to me and says something against my belief system, my religion. I will feel so offended. They too were offended, but they had the courage to go through it. They checked their assumptions and said these are valid and these are invalid. Through this process of thinking, they arrived at a pedestal of greater truth which is why they were invested in it. They made a difference just like the initial community of the Prophet. After that, we have been on the decline because we are not critical and consequently not invested in a wholesome message. We merely follow packaged religions and cultures of our birth.

We need to be very honest, sincere, and truthful about our own lives. We need to try and understand the truth for what it is worth. This requires us to be very critical of our assumptions, our history, and our theology. It requires that we arrive at a point of neutrality. When we are at a point of neutrality, we will not be perturbed when we are faced with counter arguments to the assertions that we make. It also requires us to be detached emotionally from the situation. If we are emotionally invested in a situation, we will never be able to objectively assess that situation. Our attachment, our love, our affection, and our affiliation – all these things will impact the way we are. We can never understand the way something is until we distance ourselves from it. We cannot be emotive about the truth.

I will tell you why we need to evaluate our beliefs objectively. Me and you are on a one way street. Death and our graves await us. Once the angel of death grips us, there is no coming back. At that point I will not be there for you and you will not be there for me. At that point God says, "They will find Me". It will be me and my God. Nothing else will matter. At that point I cannot give you as a reference, nor will you be able to give me as a reference. We will be told, "It was your story. You knew very well deep within you. Why did you not awaken? Why did you throw away that one and only opportunity? You have no one but yourself to blame."

God says in the Quran, "The end of man's journey will be with the Sustainer. He will be judged on that Day on what he has done and what he has left undone. He shall be a witness against himself, even though he may veil himself in excuses." (75:12-15). No excuses will work on the Day of Judgment. Instead man will say, "O Lord! We hear, and we can now see! Send us back so that we may perform righteous deeds." The response shall be, "No, your opportunity is gone! We made a certain pact, and it is finished. It is done!" Packaged religions, at times, bring about a worldview which is wholly inaccurate that we have to deconstruct by being totally open and honest.

Before we conclude today's talk, I will ask you these questions: Can there be a religion from God that does not have high regard for human values? Can there be a religion from God that does not value harmonious coexistence? Can there be a religion from God that does not value the goodness of humanity when it is directed towards God, whether that be in the name of Allah or any other name? There cannot be such a religion from God. He cannot favour one over the other. God cannot have chosen ones with guaranteed salvation. Even before the Quran tells us this, our minds will tell us that God cannot be this way. But since we are born into a packaged religion it conditions us to believe that we are the chosen ones. We are the best ones. We are going into Paradise. We do not have to do much work. Therefore, the first thing that is required here is that we become objective – brutally honest and very sincere. This is what I call the state of fluidity: meaning that we are always able to shed and accept and that nothing becomes our identity. Whatever proves itself to be worthy, we take on, and whatever proves itself to be unworthy, we can let go because we are not emotionally invested in it. In this way, we are invested in the truth alone and are brutally honest.

What can a person lose by being truthful? From the outset, you will be able to say to God, "O Lord, to the best of my ability I tried to seek You and Your good pleasure." Tell me, can you get it wrong after that? There cannot be anybody who arrives at that point of brutal honesty, sincerity, fluidity and also be wrong. You can say, "O Lord, I gave my heart to You! I sincerely tried to find You! I sincerely tried to uphold the truth in how I found it." In that way, no individual can be wrong to the extent of being committed to the truth as and how it is discovered. Two sincere individuals on the path of searching for the truth are both right despite their differences. Even if they are different in terms of arbitrary features such as the religion they follow, the culture in which they are born, their family, their status, their race and their gender; essentially they are both right since their aim is to discover the truth as it is without any bias, ego or arrogance. If a person arrives at this point, they can never be wrong after that because they are sincerely trying to find God and are open to criticism and change. That is the essential benefit of becoming fluid and objective.

What do I lose if I become objective and fluid? Nothing. On the contrary, I will find a greater truth. The only thing I will lose is a false belief that I have carried so close to my heart. If I uphold a false belief, then that is knowingly wanting to be wrong. Look at Iblis. All he had to do was to let go of his arrogance. An honest enquiry brings a sense of greater understanding of the purpose. Whenever we become honest – brutally honest – it allows us to appreciate the position of the "other" as well. Moreover, if both people become extremely honest and sincere, they find a greater truth beyond the both of them. It is not cosmetic; it is the real thing.

When I sit with the Christians, I say that I am not in this pretence business. I am not going to say something to make you feel good. I am what I am. We will share openly. Whatever Allah has given you belongs to me, and whatever little I might have belongs to you. I am not going to sit here as a "Muslim" talking to a "Christian". I am going to sit here as a humble servant and slave of God who is trying to find his God. Whatever you can give me, I will take from you. It doesn't matter to me what religion you are. Labels can be placed and removed. The real thing is what is happening inside.

When we sit with the Sunnis I say that all this talk of us "being one" is not enough. Let us debate the contentious issues that we have. If we are wrong, I will let it go. If we are right, you uphold it as well. If you have the truth, then I need to have it. If you have a point, then I need to appreciate it but let us be genuine, honest, and brutally sincere about it. And this was actually the state of the Prophet. Every prophet that came into this world was brutally honest, very sincere, and out to attain the truth. There was not a shred of arrogance inside them that they had not removed – yes, of course, as human beings they had that, but they were able to let go. The prophets therefore, questioned their assumptions.

Read what God says about Prophet Ibrahim. Read about his personal journey to find God and how he became "one of those who are inwardly sure." (6:75) Ibrahim was very truthful, honest, genuine and sincere. He looked at the star and said, "There is my God." He was going through these processes. And when the star faded away he said, "It can't be my God, it has gone away." He is very honest, sincere, truthful, and objective. He is able to critique himself. He is critically looking at the belief systems of the people that were around him. He goes through the same thought process with the moon and the sun where he momentarily entertains the prevalent beliefs and critiques them. Why do you think Allah is narrating all these beautiful things about Ibrahim? He was beautifully going through those processes within himself, very sincerely and genuinely arriving at a different rank of truth – a glorious level of truth.

He is the father of the Muslims. He is the one who has named you "those who have surrendered to God". What does surrendered to God mean? It does not mean following a system of religion. It means an intellectual and emotional surrender. Whatever God suggests to me as the truth, that has rational appeal and is right, I will accept. This is my surrender. At the level of my heart, whatever is righteous, I will accept it. I will be able to let go of my emotional attachments. That was the Islam of Ibrahim. These were the processes that this great sage of God – great friend of God – was going through, and this is required of all of us.

Now look at Imam Husayn – what a brilliant man! What a phenomenal man! Have you ever wondered why his appeal goes beyond his time and region? Have you ever wondered why he transcends cultural and religious differences? At the remembrance of Husayn, people of different religions find that their inner sentiments are reflected by the sentiments that he portrayed on that day – his dignity, calm, and surrender to God. They say that Husayn goes beyond Islam. When you go to Dar es Salaam, you find the Hindus there saying that he embraces Hinduism. When you talk to Christians, they say, "He voices our genuine intimate bonding with God." Jews, Christians, Hindus, Buddhists all love him. Why? Because he had arrived at that point of righteousness, truthfulness, sincerity, and fluidity on which he was embracing the truth as and how he found it.

That is why he is such an icon for humanity. He transcends not only colour, gender and status. He transcends religion as a whole. He is beyond religion. Husayn ibn Ali is a religion onto himself – a Godly religion. In his flock of seventy-two people you had people who were Christians or converts on the day of battle, he accepted them and they accepted him. Their Christianity was not a barrier. Imagine, they were with him and he was with them. I presume there were people who were praying with their arms folded. Did he have any concerns about that? These were secondary issues. There was something far greater to the truth that they had managed to understand.

So the charm of Husayn ibn Ali and his appeal to one and all is in essence the point that we are trying to make: finding that sense of purpose, sincerely committing to it, being invested in it, and living a life that is worthy so that at the point of death I am not bewildered, confused, or perplexed. To be able to take the last breath and say, "O Lord, I thank You for a wonderful opportunity and I thank You for coming to receive me." What a life that would be!

Night Two

We have stated that for us to live a meaningful life we need to know the purpose for which this life has been given to us. This requires that we become brutally honest and sincere in order to examine whatever it is that we understand of the truth. We are born into cultures and religions and they induce a sense of righteousness in our minds. We grow into them and never look at them critically; we never challenge them. The Quran, on the contrary, asks us to think constantly, find our way, and find a sense of purpose. The Quran asks us to critique our belief systems.

We also stated that the Quran did not ask the Meccans as Meccans to critique their cultures, their theology and the systems in which they existed. Rather, it asked the Meccans as human beings to critique, and therefore it also applies to us at present. The Quran is asking us to critique things and understand things properly. This requires a state of neutrality and fluidity. A state of fluidity means that we are not restricted or bound by anything – there is nothing sacred. There is no sacredness about anything. When we enter our graves even our bodies shall perish within a few months. The person who bestows sacredness upon other objects is not sacred himself – Think about that! The House of God, the Ka'ba, has been broken down many times in the history of its existence. It has also been burned when it was made from wood. There is no such thing as "sacredness" that we have in our minds. Sacredness is our genuine understanding of the truth and what we become through it. That is the only thing that is sacred.

To be open minded, critical and brutally honest requires us to stand away a little and not to be so emotionally attached to our religions and our cultures. When we are emotionally attached, we cannot see things for what they really are. We get hurt and offended when challenged about our beliefs. If we can somehow move back and look at things for what they are worth, we will begin to understand what is required of us in this life. If there is a purpose, then we will understand that purpose and we will be fully invested in that purpose – we will strive to attain it. When people arrive at this level of sincerity, truthfulness, honesty, questioning and enquiry, no two people can be wrong – it is amazing.

How is it possible that two people who are very different cannot be wrong? I will say the differences in this case are like the differences in our features, our genders and our social status. These differences do not really tantamount to differences in a substantive manner, do they? Two people of different genders can still both be friends of God and beloved to God because what is essential is not their features it is something else. I take this a step further and say that even religion does not determine truthfulness and righteousness. To a great extent religion is like our features and genders. It is like the clothes that we wear.

The Quran says, "The people who believe, the Jews, the Christians, and the Sabians – among them whoever believes in Allah and the Last Day, and does righteous deeds, they will have their reward with their Lord and they shall have no fear, nor shall they grieve." (2:62) The Quran is setting formalised religion as a feature that does not necessarily distinguish right from wrong at the level of assuring salvation. It is giving centrality to God, a sense of purpose through righteous deeds and a sense of responsibility through the notion of the Hereafter. So, if a person can arrive at a state of brutal honesty and be able to critique whatever they find, whatever they assume to be the truth, whatever they have grown into; such a person can never be wrong. Such a person, as we will explain afterwards, is on the path of self-realisation and evolutionary growth. Ponder on the Quranic verse. It is like saying I read this text book but he read that text book and yet both of us passed the exam.

When a person is honest and saying to God, O Lord, I genuinely am searching for You. I have not allowed my own ego, arrogance, and likes and dislikes to prevail beyond You. Then wherever you arrive in that state of sincerity, you are truthful and have attained your purpose. Anybody who arrives at this level of truthfulness of enquiry, critique, and sincerity can never be wrong, and through this level of honesty we begin to respect each other. In fact, we ask God, O Lord, You have created such a beautiful earth for us. The mass of water and wood is balanced so beautifully that it allows us to sail and go from one continent to another. You knew what our burdens would be, thus you created the camel to carry our burdens and the cow to give us milk. All of it was ready made for us. O Lord, how is it possible that after making such a beautiful earth and creating upon it human beings, You would want to destroy all of them and save only a handful? It does not make sense.

In fact, if you look at the Quran you will notice this trend. In the case of Prophet Nuh the majority of the people who were alive were destroyed, and in the case of Prophet Hud and Saleh the majority of the people were destroyed. In the case of Prophet Lut the majority of the people were destroyed. But with the passage of time, we find less and less people are being destroyed. In the case of Prophet Muhammad nobody was destroyed. Even his bitter opponents, the worst of God's creatures, were mostly saved with only a few killed in warfare. We say O God, it doesn't make sense that You want to destroy everyone.

What would be the result if we were brutally honest and critical? You see, sometimes we are baffled by the "other" and we say how can other people make such claims? Why aren't they critical about the claims they are making? Here is an invitation for me and you to introspect and to try to understand things accurately. There are two things we need to realise. Firstly, we need to genuinely try and understand the claim others are making on their own terms. Secondly, we have to assess whether we are guilty of doing the same thing we are accusing others of doing.

The initial reaction to others is that what they are saying is absurd. This reaction makes us arrogant of our own position – it stifles us. We are uncritical of our own position because we, as an implication of the rejection of their position, accept our own without investigation. For instance, the Christians advocate a trinitarian theology. We believe that they are *mushriks*, those who ascribe partners to God, but when we ask them they insist that they are not *mushriks*. How interesting is this? We call them *mushrik* and they respond that you have not understood the notion of trinity the way we have understood it. If a person was brutally honest and truthful, they would want to examine the claims of others from their own perspective.

How interesting is this that the Quran does not call them *mushrik*? The Quran calls them *ahl al-kitāb* (the people of the Book) but at the same time it points out to the Christians that this is a form of *kufr* (disbelief) but it does not label them *mushrik*. It is trying to reason with them. How beautifully Allah does things, He praises the Christians in the Quran but at the same time He says this is a form of *kufr*. When the Jews say that they are the chosen ones, the Quran frowns upon this. The amazing thing is that the Quran calls them the chosen ones. God says, "We gave preference to the Israelites over the people of the worlds." (2:47) On the one hand they have been chosen, and on the other they have been frowned upon. So, we need to understand things accurately and carefully.

Other sects of Islam may label Shia Muslims as *mushrik*. They may say you touch the Ka'ba, kiss the black stone, touch the tomb of the Prophet and Imams – this is *shirk*, this is ascribing partners to God. The response of the Shia is that you have not understood us properly. This is not a form of *shirk*. Some may call me a *mushrik* for wearing this ring if I become insecure when this ring is taken off! They would tell me that I am engaging in a form of *shirk*. I would rebuttal and say well you don't understand my position with regard to the meaning of *shirk*.

Do we not have this notion as Muslims that we are the chosen ones? That we are being favoured. That God has favoured us. We thank Allah for giving us birth in Islam, don't we? We thank Allah for being the lovers of Muhammad, the Messenger, and Imam Ali. Do we not thank God for favouring us? The Jews do the same; they are thanking God for favouring them. What is the difference between what the Jews are doing and what we are doing? Are we not the ones whose salvation is guaranteed; are we not the chosen ones?

The whole journey of man was not intended to simply receive answers from others. The journey is one of continual questioning and striving, and the answers are supposed to be arrived at. This is why the Muslim minds are so lazy. The pulpit forces "truth" down people's throats. The Quran did not do this. What did the Quran state? It invites people to think. "Think about what you are believing in." "Had there been within the heavens and earth gods besides Allah, they both would have been ruined." (21:22) "Do you not see the sailing ship, the rising sun, and the luminous stars? Is there not a sign in there for you to awaken?" It is all about becoming inquisitive and questioning.

At this juncture, we will clarify this notion of the "chosen ones". We know people are chosen. The problem is that we have not understood it accurately. I can choose anyone here to perform a task but that does not mean that they are guaranteed success. They have a certain aptitude through which they become eligible for a certain task but that does not mean they are favoured. Nor does it mean that they are guaranteed success or salvation, in that is their test. So "the chosen ones" means that some people who have specific attributes in a particular location are taken up to perform certain tasks – that is it.

It does not mean that they are favoured ones of God or that God is going to overlook their wrongs. No, every one of them has their journey and test. So, there is no chosen one in the sense of one being favoured by God, for whose wrongdoings God is going to turn a blind eye, and that they can do whatever they want. God says this in the Quran to the Jews that "If you say that you are the sons of God then why does God punish you?" (5:18) They have totally misunderstood the meaning of the "chosen ones" – it does not mean that. We should totally dispel this notion from our minds. Just because we are born within the folds of Islam does not mean that we are guaranteed salvation.

Salvation is something totally different, in that it's in our hands entirely and subject to our own efforts. There is one thing God has not determined and that is individual salvation. We either attain it or we don't. The Prophet of God said, "Each one of you simultaneously has a place in heaven and hell. You will acquire one over the other through the journey of life. If you acquire heaven, you have left hell. If you acquire hell, you have vacated heaven." Simultaneously there are two places for everyone. It is undetermined whether it will be heaven or hell. The notion of "the chosen one" is other than salvation or the favoured one.

So, we come to this understanding that we need to be fully objective, and we reserve the right to question with brutal honesty in a state of fluidity. That which we understand determines the degree to which we are invested in this life. The first principle we arrive at, before we begin to question our assumptions, is that I am responsible for my life, and responsibility cannot be shifted upon the shoulders of another. If you read the Quran, it says that all will face God individually on the Day of Judgement *(qiyāma)* and none will be spared.

When we read at the Quran we find that God will question prophet Isa too. "O Isa ibn Maryam, did you say to the people worship me and my mother?" (5:116) If God is going to question Isa, who is ranked amongst the greatest of prophets alongside Prophet Muhammad and Ibrahim, then do you think God is not going to question us? If God is not going to spare Isa, do you think He will spare us? He is not. We need to be very clear about this: there is a burden of responsibility on our shoulders individually that cannot be shifted onto the shoulders of another. What have you done and what have you become? It was your life. It was your opportunity. What did you make of it?

God says, "Did I not enjoin on you, O you children of Adam, that you should not worship Satan – since, verily, he is your open foe." (36:60) God keeps reminding us, "At an individual level you are responsible to Me. We made a pact so you are responsible." If we put the Quran aside and look deep into ourselves, what will we find? We will find that we are vested with responsibility that we cannot shift. If I go to the court for speeding and the judge asks, "Why did you speed? 120 mph is hazardous" and I reply, "Zayd was speeding, that is why." The judge would exclaim, "What? We are going to jail you with Zayd. If you are going to follow him on the motorway, you might as well follow him into the dungeons." The Quran repeatedly asks why did you do this? The people reply that our elders did it. The Quran exclaims burn with them then!" God will say burn in hell with them!"

So, we have this responsibility that we cannot shift onto anybody else's shoulders. The first thing that God will say to us is why did you not think? I gave you a brain! I gave you an opportunity. I spoke to you in My Quran. I spoke to you within your soul to think. Think! Does this make sense? What is going on? You failed to think! You let others think for you. They have failed miserably, and you failed with them.

You are responsible for your own self. Show me where in the Book of God the Quranic sentiment is inconsistent with the human sentiment? The human sentiment is that every person is responsible for what they do. They cannot shift the burden of responsibility onto another. Tell me one verse of the Quran in which Allah allows us to shift the burden of responsibility from our shoulders to somebody else's. Nowhere! That is the sentiment with which the Quran empowers people. You are responsible for your life. You will find God at the end of the journey and He will question you. It will be a story between you and your Lord. The first thing we need to understand is that we are responsible. No one else is going to bear our responsibility.

Now, we go into the first assumption: is there a purpose? Is there a purpose to life or have I just taken birth into a religion and a culture that has induced in my mind that there is a purpose? Is there a God or have I just become conditioned to believe that there is a God? Now these questions might be startling. You may be thinking how can a lecturer ask, from the pulpit, if there is a God? Seriously? The pulpit is not supposed to ask such a question; the pulpit is supposed to assume. But the topic is checking our assumptions. And if I were to ask, is there a God, the first one to commend me would be God Himself for asking such a question.

Is there a purpose? Let us go into this question and in our investigation we will take aid of the Quran as well. If we observe the human community, it is obvious that there is a collective purpose, either advertently or inadvertently. What is that purpose? We are intellectually and technologically evolving. We want to know things, explore, learn, to know whether things constitute purposes or not. Knowing, exploring and uncovering the nature of reality is definitely a purpose. Evolving and exploiting nature is a purpose. What drives us into deep space? Why do we want to know the beginnings of the physical universe? Why do we want to discover the cosmic microwave background from the big bang? Why do we want to know whether this universe is the product of another collapsed universe? Why do we have a theory that this universe is connected through an umbilical cord to another universe? Are we ever going to go into another universe? The big bang happened billions of years ago, is it of any use for us to know this? Yet we want to know, do we not? We want to discover and we want to know. There is this yearning and thirst inside us to know. So immediately we know that knowing, discovering and evolving intellectually is definitely a purpose.

We want to grow and we want to mature intellectually. We have to be inquisitive and ask what is the meaning of this? What is the connection between the growing crop and the rising sun and the descending rain showers? What is the connection between these natural phenomena? And after discovering, how beautifully we can make use of it all. The early man was inquisitive. They discovered things that we are still using today. That definitely is a purpose. The Quran states, "And He taught Adam the names of all things." (2:31) There is something in our nature that compels us to want to know. We want to know and we want to discover. So, knowing is intrinsic to whatever purpose we have.

Another thing that is happening to the human community is that we are becoming morally righteous. In today's world we all know that giving life is better than taking life. In fact, we will not be tolerant of nations that are not upholding the human rights of their own subjects. We went to war against Gaddafi with the pretext that he was not upholding the human rights of his own subjects. We marched in the streets of London protesting our government's decision to go to war with Iraq because it was inconsistent with human rights. We are becoming morally refined. We are now collectively agreeing that there are inalienable human rights. We are seeing their moral basis. We understand that we must speak the truth. We understand that when we transact there must be justice and fairness. We understand that life is sacred. We understand that charity is good. We understand goodness is something that is preferred. From this we deduce that we are morally evolving, and the Quran is helping us. Here, I should point out that if we look at the Quranic message, there are moral codes scattered within its verses that appeal to humanity at large, regardless of whether people are spiritually inclined or not. They appeal to one and all!

Then there is another level in terms of our purpose, and it is something that the Quran talks about. It is something that is eating away at us. The feeling that there has to be something deeper to it all and there has to be a more profound meaning. There has to be an intimate belonging. I need to find myself. This is resonated by the Quran, "O my servant who has attained inner peace, return to your Sustainer." (89:27-28) These verses, and others, such as, "*Innā lillāh wa innā ilayhi raji'ūn* – Indeed, we are from Allah and to Him shall we return," (2:156) are awakening that deep level of purpose within us. Undoubtedly, there is intellectual evolution and moral evolution, both of which inform us of a purpose, but all of these seem to be very superficial. Neither of them satiate us. There is nothing that will give us satisfaction until we arrive at that deep-seated level of existence and purpose. A state where our humanity realises itself fully and substantively.

This level of purpose requires us to awaken to ourselves and recognise ourselves for what we are. It requires us to be liberated from all inner obstacles and grow to a state of inner completion. This is only possible when we surrender to God intimately since God marks the peak of our aspirations. Through Him we remove our state of inner lack and arrive at our completion and mirror His beauty and perfection. Only an intimate belonging with Him and surrender to Him will bring us to the fullness of our existence. This requires us to understand certain things. If there is a God, what is the nature of God and what is His relationship with us?

Now, think about these three levels of purpose that we have talked of. The first two, the intellectual and moral purpose that are resulting in intellectual and moral evolution, are present within the human community whether people choose to believe in God or not. In reality, they cannot exist without God but because naïve people think intellectual and moral evolution can exist without God let us assume the first two purposes exist without God. What about the third one? That deep-seated spiritual need and want to belong and grow through. The need for meaning in life and substantive existence; what about that one? So I ask you, is there a purpose? We are seeing that there is a purpose.

The third level of purpose leads us to question our fundamental assumption: is there a God? Now tell me, if each one of us were to discover deep within ourselves – truthfully – that there is a God, how invested we would become in that purpose? Imagine if we can go beyond that God who we only pray to formally to the God within, with whom we live, breathe and talk. Imagine if I can arrive at a God that exists with me. As He says, "He is with you wherever you may be, and He sees all that you do." (57:4)

Imagine if I can arrive at that understanding of God who sees what is going on deep within my heart. Imagine if I understand a God to Whom I can say "*Allahumma tawakkaltu alayk* – O Lord, I am relying on You." Imagine if there was a belonging to a God to Whom I can say, "*Lā ḥawla wa lā quwwata illā billāh* – There is no ability and there is no strength, except through Allah." Imagine if I were to find the God of Husayn! What God did he have whereby he has a smile under the blade? The blade appears upon his neck and the smile appears upon his lips - imagine!

So here we ask is there a God? And if there is a God what type of God is He? What is His relationship with me? It is here and now that I can make that genuine enquiry, "O God, are You?" I will say straight off that none of the traditional theological and philosophical arguments for the existence of God satisfy – none of them. To me, they are all redundant. There is not a single argument where we cannot knock great holes in, and that is why I am saying that the God that is found through formal theology is not a real God. No wonder He does not give that sense of substantive existence, that sense of real being. Imagine, if I find my God, do you think I would be at this despicable level of existence in which I am swearing at the majority of Muslims?

NIGHT TWO

In which babies are dying and I sleep peacefully? Really?

Do you think that if I found my God I would be filled with so much anxiety and fear? Do you think if I found my God I would be carrying the burdens of life on my shoulders? I will put them in the hands of God. God, You are my parent. You are my Master. You are my Lord. You are my everything. With You as my God, why am I worried? If You take me, who can save me? Why should I worry about life and death? If You keep me hungry, who can feed me? If You feed me, who can snatch it away from me? Imagine how liberating that would be? Imagine the God that Imam Ali talks about, "O God, who do I have but You?" That intimate belonging.

We all say that there is a God, but the question is what is God? It is like saying there is Mount Everest, but what does Everest mean to us? A building down the road? If you believe that to be the Everest, it is not Everest. The same is the case with God. There is a God. That's the God I need to pray to and He will reward me like a headmaster. Is God like a headmaster? Or is there an intimate belonging with God? A deep-seated purpose and meaning with God? This is the first assumption. Now suppose, if we were to find through a genuine enquiry that there is a God at our personal level and that He is a loving and caring God, a God that liberates us, wants us to grow, and wants us to belong to Him. Imagine after that how deep our sense of purpose would become? How meaningful existence would become? How worthy every breath would become? You know the worth of a breath cannot be known until it begins to get snatched from us. That is when we understand the worth of a breath, otherwise we will not. We have so many of these breaths, and look at how these breaths are being wasted. There is no purpose to them.

Imagine if I were to find my God – if we were to find our sense of God – how uncomplicated this life would become. If I found God He will relieve me of my fear. The reason why I do not ask questions is because I am fearful that asking these questions will make me into a disbeliever. We are told that these questions are from Shayṭān (Satan). If that is the case then Shayṭān is the biggest mercy. If Shayṭān is putting these questions in our minds, then that is the reason Shayṭān was created: to ignite our minds and to bring about growth within us. That is a wonderful purpose that Shayṭān is serving if that is what Shayṭān is doing. The same God who we fear to pose questions of encourages us to question. There are many occasions in which we experience certain emotions and entertain questions but then immediately shun them away. We repent and say *astaghfirullah, astaghfirullah*. But a true man of God will say the fact that this question has come to my mind means that I should think about it. No matter how despicable the thought I am going to introspect. Let me think about this question and grow through it. In this way, God becomes a force of growth and liberation.

These are the beautiful days of the beautiful man – the one who is among the most liberated of men. Look at the way he understands God. In his supplication, he gestures and says, "O Allah, I have now begun to see that every event of life was constructed with the particular aim of You introducing Yourself to me." What he is saying is that everything in life was geared towards one thing: finding God in the most accurate manner, in the most substantive manner. Imagine if a person were to ask the question is there a God, and if so, then O Lord, how are You? If there is a genuine enquiry and a person finds God, imagine how liberating that can be!

Night Three

We stated previously that we need to critically evaluate our assumptions in order to get an accurate understanding of what we are all about, and what life is all about. For that, we need to have a free hand and be confident about ourselves. We need to know that it is our God-given right to question our assumptions. No one can dictate anything to anybody else. I need to arrive at my own truth and I have a stake-holding in what I believe. That will motivate and drive me to lead a meaningful life as opposed to just existing. I will be substantively living – achieving a purpose by being invested in what I commit myself to.

The first assumption was: is there a purpose? We discussed that we see a purpose at different levels, but there is an inner calling to find a deep-seated meaning from within that would satiate and fulfil us- give us security and satisfaction. We also stated that if each one of us as individuals, as we will elaborate further today, arrives at that point of brutal honesty, enquiry, critique and sincerity, then we will have our own truth. However, we will all be the same and none of us will be wrong. The blessed Prophet said that "Salman is on tenth rank of faith whilst Abu Dharr is on the ninth rank of faith. If Abu Dharr were to know what is deep within the heart of Salman he would declare Salman a disbeliever, or he would put Salman to death thinking that Salman was an apostate or something other than a Muslim." Yet the Prophet, in the same breath, said that paradise eagerly awaits both Salman and Abu Dharr. Both are very different and both have found different routes to the truth. But both are equally right in their own way because both have arrived at that point of sincerity, brutal honesty, and fluidity in embracing the truth as they find it.

We said that the third level of purpose that requires us to have a deep-seated meaning and a real sense of life is connected with the existence of God. If we take God out of the picture, then that very deep sense of purpose and meaning does not seem to exist. I will just point to this as we elaborate. With God comes the notion of real responsibility, of questioning in the Hereafter, and of reward and punishment. There is also a deep recognition that He is nurturing us and knows us well. Only with God does that real sense of purpose come to the hearts and minds of individuals. Therefore, the first thing we need to ask is: is there a God? We need to check this assumption. We stated that the traditional theological arguments that try to validate the existence of God fail miserably. Even the philosophical arguments really do not make much sense apart from what the *Sadrian* philosophy advances in terms of "unity of being and its gradational descent".

The real answer that you and I find is that of course there is a God. The simplest answer is that I know this from the depth of my heart. The fact that I have opened my eyes in this beautiful universe and I have been awoken. The fact that I see around myself a pre-existing universe that has already awoken to itself without me awakening it, shows that there is a greater sense of awakening that precedes me, which has awoken me, and is in a state of perfect harmony and beautifully balanced, it is a display of an ineffable being conscious of itself. As far as God is concerned, the answer comes from within: He is, and He is the Absolute Being. He does not need to be proven. The God of the traditional theologians is the God of the mind. He does not fulfil us. He is a God that is an intellectual God. We are talking about the real sense of God, the God of the mystics. They are the people who say He is. Try to understand how He is. As the Imam says, "Nobody knows how He is save Himself." It was never a question of proving that God exists. And that is why the Quran always says, "There are signs in this for those who reflect."

Allah states, "And among His Signs is the creation of the heavens and the earth, and the variations in your languages and your colours. Verily in that are Signs for those who know." (30:22) Here the Quran is not presenting philosophical and logical arguments. It is merely teasing the mind, saying to the mind think – something is going on. Such meticulous working of the beautiful system shows that it is alive to itself. So, is there a God? The answer is a resounding yes, there is! You and I call Him "God". Some people might call it "nature". Others might call it "the cosmic consciousness". Me and you will call Him "the Most Merciful". After acknowledging that there is God and after arriving at this understanding that there is some expectation from me in this life, imagine how meaningfully that contributes towards the formation of a purpose. Imagine how intense the individual investment into that purpose will be.

Now we ask what is the nature of this God? Is He an impersonal God who is not involved with me, who I cannot approach? We know there is some responsibility towards Him, and that we cannot shift our responsibilities upon the shoulders of others because I, myself, am living this life. This life is about me. Trying to understand the nature of God, as accurately as possible, will determine our outlook on life, on how we understand life. This will then determine how we behave in our lives in our individual capacities and in our collective capacities.

Imagine if a person has this notion that he is the favoured one of God and that God will overlook all his faults. Of course, such a person will turn out to be a monstrous person in the name of God. With this attitude the production of ISIS is a natural outcome as is the production of the Zionist state, in which many do not care about the dying children in Palestine. Such a sense of

God allows them to commit indescribable crimes and transgressions in the name of God despite it not being right within itself, and despite it not feeling right within the core of their being. Imagine if I believe in a God who has favoured me, then it is very easy for me to point a finger at the "other", pronounce that they are wrong, and de-humanise them.

Our sense of God will determine how we become from within, how we lead our lives. So here it is: if God is a transcendent God, one who sits upon a throne, who is so lofty, so majestic, that He is unapproachable; then of course that personal relationship with God, that intimate bonding with God, is out of the question all together. This will naturally cause feelings of unworthiness within my soul, and consequently, I need somebody else that is an intermediary between me and my God. Thus, God becomes totally unapproachable. If the notion of God is that He is a tyrannical God – vengeful, unforgiving and uncompromising, the one who will bring you to question for every single detail, then that will be reflected in our social, legal, political and religious outlooks.

If we teach in our religious schools (*madrasa*) that you need to fear God, the lofty God; He is so mighty; He will not forgive you for anything, then of course we will feel unworthy within ourselves. And if God is so vengeful, wrathful, and unforgiving, then of course I will state, "If you perform ablution (*wuḍū'*) and one millimetre of your arm is not washed, then your prayer is not accepted." Naturally, it will lead me to these conclusions. I will teach in madrasa the fear of God as opposed to belonging to God and loving God. My sense of God will determine what I become because I will emulate God.

How wonderful is the story of Shams Tabrizi when he was sitting in the company of scholars as they spoke of the obligatory acts. How uncompromisingly they spoke, "Such and such an act is not accepted unless it is performed with such and such a form." He said, "Indeed, you worship a wrathful God and He will punish you because you are punishing yourselves." The way in which we understand God determines the way in which we become ourselves. If God is so authoritarian that He does not allow questioning of Him, then of course our religion will teach us that to question is to sin. How odd is the story of the son of Adam who behaves in contradiction to his own nature? When the spirit of God was breathed into Adam and the angels were told to prostate in front of him they protested. According to a narration, they said, "Why did You choose him? Why did You teach him the names? Why not us?" A response came, "He asked Me what these things are? They have always been around you, yet you have never asked Me. He has that inside him. He has that inquisitive nature that you do not have, which makes him eligible." How inconsistent is our belief of the God who dare not be questioned with the intrinsic nature that God has vested in us of inquisitiveness?

Look at the Quran where the angels were protesting and questioning God, "Will you place someone on the earth who will spread corruption and bloodshed, whereas we are the ones who worship You and glorify You?" (2:30) God could have easily silenced them, could He not? He could have said I know more than you, which He did. But then He engaged with the angels and provided the reason for choosing Adam. This is a very different God to the one that I worship. If God is so transcendent, His majesty so lofty that I cannot reach Him and I cannot question Him, then the attitude would be the same attitude as the one we see in the religious community. The attitude that do not question what comes in the name of religion. Your task is to follow it. Your task is not to question.

If I do not question, in the first instance, why would I be drawn to that religion? If I do not ask or I do not get satisfactory answers, then why should I come to that religion in the first place? It is a very simple thing; I need to ask. I could have been born a Christian, or a Jew, or a Hindu, or a Buddhist. How can you blame the Christians, the Jews, the Hindus and the Buddhists for following their faiths? You do not allow your community to ask; they do not allow their communities to ask. And then you fight with each other in the name of your Gods who say, "I am one God!" Yet, you make Him into many other Gods and then you kill each other. Does that really make sense? So, the understanding of God impacts us in the most intimate way. It determines what we become, and the sort of life that we will lead.

Now, if we look at God from deep within our human condition and from the Quran , we might find a very different God – a God that is far more human-friendly. If we look deep into ourselves and ask God, what do You need from me? But I know that if You are God, then by priority You are needless. I know that needlessness means: You can love without wanting back; You can give without taking; You can forgive without punishing. For these are the states of completion that You have inspired me with. Every human being will state that to forgive is better than to punish, to give life is better than to take life, to be emotionally detached from the situation is better than to be involved in a petty situation, to show that you are greater person is better than to fall to the level of the antagonist who is not so human. If this is the sense of righteousness that You, O God, have instilled inside me, then by priority You ought to have all of that. If You have created my mother with blind love towards me, then surely this blindness of love is an aspect of Your own being.

So, I say to God that more than my needs towards You at a physical level, I truly need You at an intimate emotional level. There are things inside me I cannot share with anybody. I am a very private person. My mother claims to have given birth to me, nurtured me in her lap, and fed me through her own being. She assumes to know me but she does not know who I really am. I need somebody who truly knows me the way I am, in front of whom I need not feel embarrassed. At that level, I need somebody who can understand my state of insecurity, my state of apprehension, anxiety and fear; who can accept my flaws, and accept me at that level for who and what I am. I need that sort of a God so that I can go to Him, and He will embrace me and accept me as and how I am. And indeed, if You are God, then You have to be the God that I need because the distinction that You have marked between Yourself and Your creation is one of needlessness and need. You say that You are needless in the Quran .

My greatest want is this deep-seated need that I have to share, that I need to belong. I need somebody at that intimate level with me, who understands me and accepts me as I am. By merely observing my own human condition, without looking at the Quran or without any rational argument, this is evident to me. Look at the beautiful journey of Ibrahim, at every level he finds God. He says to God, "Allow me to submit to You not only intellectually but emotionally in the way You understand me, where You know me so fully." Look at how Moses unashamedly says to God, "Show me Yourself. I want to see You!" Would anybody dare utter the statement, my Lord, show me Yourself, I want to see You? This is a great Prophet saying this to God. He is sharing at that depth of his humanity. God then reveals Himself to Moses in a way that is not physical – we all know the story.

God says in the Quran, introducing His own beautiful self, "He is the First and the Last, and the Outward as well as the Inward: and He has full knowledge of everything." (57:3) He is introducing Himself in a way unknown to the traditional theologians. He is saying, "It is but Me, the entirety of the beauty that you find around you. This awakening that You have, it is nothing but Me. Try and feel Me. Yearn Me. Seek Me. Find Me. For that is your calling within yourself." Imagine if a soul were to find a God who is the Apparent and the Hidden, the One who is found everywhere you turn. Imagine if a soul were to find that God! How complete that soul would be?

Allah says, "I forgive all sins, so do not be hopeless of My mercy". He says, "O servants of Mine who have transgressed against your own selves, do not despair of God's mercy. Behold, God forgives all sins (39:53) "Do not commit a crime, do not fornicate, kill, cheat and lie. Anybody who does this shall have double the share of punishment. As for those who repent, bring faith, perform righteous deeds; I may turn their evils into good deeds." (25:70) This is how He introduces Himself. He is a very imminent God, a God that is present at all points. We ask, "O Lord, is there anything else through which You want to introduce Yourself?" And He replies, "I am your Lord. I am your *rabb*". This is the mother of all names and amongst His loftiest of names. *Rabb* is the One who nurtures. In Arabic, a housewife is called "*rabbat al-bayt*", which means the Lord of the House. She is called Lord of the House because she upholds the whole household and its needs. God is *rabb*, the One who completes us. How? He completes us in our physical being, our intellectual capacity, our emotional capacity, and our spiritual being. He introduces Himself as *rabb*, and He rejoices in the growth of His creation.

I always say that if we want to understand the nature of God, we must look into our own nature. Our nature will reveal the nature of God because an author always projects his own thoughts in his writing. A painter projects his own imaginations upon the canvass. You can see the mind of the author from the writing and you can see the mind of the artist from the painting. You can understand the nature of God from our nature. What is our nature? To bring everything to its completion. Our completion lies in us being liberated and God is the One who has the task of liberating us. God encourages questioning. He encourages rejection and acknowledgement after understanding.

I often remark, is it not a wonder that the *kalimah* begins with *lā ilāha*, there is no God? It starts with negation, with questioning. This rejection then allows for completion. God encourages this process. God is the force of liberation. He liberates us intellectually and emotionally. Have you ever wondered why we go around the Ka'ba, performing tawaf? It is done to break the psychological and intellectual idols, to break away from everything we hold as sacred in order to arrive at God in the most glorious way. God does not frown upon being questioned. God has given us this nature of questioning. He encourages questioning.

If there is God, then He has to be a God who is meaningful. O Lord, what good are You to me if I can't reach You? What good are You to me if You do not allow me to question You? What good are You to me sitting so far away upon a throne merely to bring out a book on the Day of Judgement and inform me of what I have done? O Lord, I have greater expectations from You than this! I cannot worship such a God. If You are such a God, then You are not worthy of being God. I need a God that is here with me. O Lord, by Your might I swear that You will not need to put me inside the pit of hell; I will embrace the fire myself. If I have not loved You enough, then I belong in the pit of Hell. It is like me saying to my mother that O mother, I would much rather be punished than to disappoint you. O Lord, this is the God that I need. The One that I love; the One who loves me back; the One who cares for me. The One who I can question and ask why did you do this? O Lord, I do not understand this! O Lord, this does not make sense to me! I do not need an insecure God who cannot withstand questioning.

So, God needs to be found. What is the nature of God? What is His relationship with mankind? You will find that the nature of God is that He is most loving and He is nurturing at every level. God says in the Quran, "Verily, We have created man, and We know what his innermost self whispers for We are closer to him than his jugular-vein." (50:16) He says, "Know that God intervenes between man and his heart, and that to Him you shall return." (8:24) Allah comes between a man and his own soul—his own heart. I will say O Lord, O the One who is so proximate to me, let me belong to You. And this is what it says in the Quran, "God is a companion to those who have faith, taking them out of deep darkness into the light." (2:257)

So, God is the One who nurtures us and this nurturing occurs through Him liberating us. This is what He says in the Quran that He sent His prophet who ordained good and prohibited evil, and through that He broke the shackles that tied them. He lifted the weight from their shoulders that pinned them to the ground. He liberated them. This is the God that introduces Himself within the Quran. Of course, if we look at our nature, every instructor wants their student to graduate. The instructor rejoices in the student asking questions. Every parent wants their child to come of age and to allow them to retire. How can God have a different nature to this? God wants us to come of age; He wants us to graduate. Trust me, seven billion people prostrating to God will not increase God in His authority even an iota. Seven billion people rejecting faith in God will not reduce God from his godliness even an iota. Even if the grand Gabriel were to reject God, it would not matter to God, for running away from God is to arrive at God. In His disobedience is obedience. He is that grand! That is God; He is inescapable! Even Shaytan's defiance was an acknowledgement of God. This is how phenomenal God is.

God introduces himself to us in a very meaningful and intimate way, and says, "God does not ordain indecency and injustice. He ordains righteousness and goodness to others. He ordains us to forgive; He ordains us to give life; He ordains us to be truthful." (16:90) Imagine if that is the God we believe in, how invested we would become in a righteous life? It would remove our insecurities. It would remove our hatred. How beautifully God says in the Quran, "But good and evil cannot be equal, repel evil with something that is better and reconcile with those with whom there is enmity." (41:34) If somebody is at that despicable level, you are advised to rise above and beyond it. Don't judge them but be kind to them so they too become elevated. How beautifully God teaches this in the Quran, all the beautiful human morals He gives to us and that sense of intimate belonging with God, which nurtures the soul in godliness. Then there is that spiritual connection with God, that liberated state within the mind where we can question each and everything without any fear but a guarantee of arrival at success.

God states, both from deep within our nature and the Quran, that He rejoices in our individuality and the state of relativity that is manifest. By individuality, what do we mean? If you read the Quran, you will see this human condition and sentiment reflected within it, "We gave some of Our Messengers preference over others. To some of them God spoke and He raised the rank of some others. We gave authoritative proofs to Jesus, son of Mary, and supported him by the Holy Spirit." (2:253) And He says, " We preferred some of the prophets above others, and unto David We gave the Psalms." (17:55) Here is relativity. At one point He says, "We do not distinguish between any of the messengers", and at another point He says, "We have given preference to some over others." At one level, they are all the same. Yet at another level, they are very different.

Read the Quran, it mentions the Lord of Musa, the Lord of Ibrahim, the Lord of Isa. God is talking about the state of individuality and relativity. Every individual has a unique relation to the One God. My God need not be the same God as your God (of course there is One God, what I mean is our relation to that God.) It is like having one mother who is the same for all, but we all relate to her in a very individualistic and different way, do we not? We all have very different gestures of love towards our mother. The same mother, yet we all have a very different and unique bond with her, and the mother acknowledges all of them equally. God encourages this individuality and He rejoices in this relativity, where each and every one of us have a free hand in trying to understand who He is, and forge a relationship with Him and lead our lives accordingly.

What do we find when we check our assumptions? The first question to ask is whether there is a God? The answer we will arrive at is yes there is. What is the nature of this God? It is a very kind and nurturing nature. Is it a uniform journey? No, it is an individualistic journey; find your own God. You cannot know my God and I cannot know your God. In opposition to this, is the "religious" attitude. Pray your *ṣalāh* (daily prayers) – there is no sense of finding God during it but you have done your duty. Make sure you fast – there is no sense of God during it but you have done your duty. Go around the House of God seven times. We call it the 'House of God' but God calls it the 'House of mankind' more times than His House in His book. "Behold, the first Temple ever set up for mankind was indeed the one at Bakkah: rich in blessing, and a source of guidance unto all the world." (3:96) In any case, Go around the House seven times – there is no sense of God during it but you have done your duty in a mechanical robotic fashion.

This is the attitude of "religious people". I have paid my dues. The relationship with God is not one of an employer with the employee. It is not! You have done your work for the day, now go home. No, the relationship with God is an intimate relationship of the soul. It is the affair of the heart. That is why God says "Whether by night or by day, remember your Sustainer's name, and devote yourself to Him with utter devotion" (73:8) Devotion does not mean this *ruku* (bowing) and this *sajda* (prostration), going around the Ka'ba, running between *Safa* and *Marwa*. Devotion means what Qays portrayed for his Layla, "I am totally invested in You; I am terribly in love with You; I see You and I breathe You; I uphold You above myself; I lose myself in You and I grow through You." At that point, one *sajda* weighs more than all of the devotions of the angels put together because it is the *sajda* of adoration. That devotion is asked for in order to bring about that very intimate, loving and caring relationship with God in which the soul says O Lord, if it is pleasing to You, then I shall commit myself to it.

So, God is the liberator and the nurturer. He appreciates this individuality and its relativity. No two souls can be the same and every individual needs to tread this path individually. No two people are the same and no two individuals' relationship with God is the same. It is not right for me to subscribe to the God of the Quran and not find Him within me. If I have not found Him within me, then I have not found Him at all no matter how much Quran I read. It is no good for me to recite prayers after prayers if I do not find the One I am devoting myself to. It is no good doing this *wuḍū'* and this *ṣalāh* if it is not with the sentiment of devoting ourselves to Allah.

On that point I want to say something about *dua* (supplications). The supplications that we read should come from within. "I am calling You, my Lord!" *Dua Kumayl* is Imam Ali ibn Abi Talib's devotion to God. It becomes my devotion when I relate to it. The most pleasing dua to God is the one that comes from me, myself. A parrot can read the entire supplication. It will not mean anything. A child can mimic the older brother. It does not mean anything. But when the child comes to the parent with his own broken words and says something to the parent, the parent rejoices, "He/she is saying it of their own accord. They mean it. They are here they are in front of me. It is no longer a tape recorder saying it! It is the person saying it!" That is the individuality that we need. O Lord, I am not as eloquent as Your Ali, and who can be? I will talk to You in my own language, through my own broken words. I am not articulate, but You know what is in my heart. O Lord, this is the pain through which I call You. This is the hope through which I yearn You. This is the anxiety with which I come to Your door. This is the God that needs to be found, and once we find that God, imagine!

Imagine if we can find that liberating God that unshackles us at an intellectual level. Imagine how confident and empowered the individual becomes. If a person finds that God at an emotional level, imagine how complete that soul becomes, how fearless that soul becomes. Most of the time we are seeking validity from others. We want others to validate us. Validation should come only from God and nobody else. Anybody else's validation does not mean anything. It does not even matter. God frees human beings from pretentiousness and brings them into a sense of real existence and makes their lives worthwhile. These were the lives that were led by these people of Karbala whose mention we make in these blessed nights.

Night Four

When we critically evaluate our lives, we discover that there is a definite purpose and that purpose naturally is our intellectual completion, moral refinement and a deep-seated spiritual fulfilment. The third aspect, that deep-seated want to be fulfilled spiritually and to have a real sense of existence, is what truly constitutes the purpose. That is intimately connected with none other than the existence of God. So, the question that we need to ask is: is there a God, and if so, what is the nature of God? We have already stated, yes there is a God. We feel God. God is inescapable and beyond logical arguments. The Quran beautifully says, "There are signs in this for those who think." "Know that God gives life to the earth after it has been lifeless! We have indeed made Our messages clear unto you, so that you might use your reason." (57:17)

Signs are unlike logical demonstrations that are rationally based in black and white. Signs are things that appeal to us at an individual subjective level. We not only reason with them but also feel through them, there is an emotional factor attached to them. Signs allow us to find God through ourselves – a real God. The God of the traditional theologians is a God of the mind alone. He gives us a vague concept that He is there but does not motivate us. The God of a lover, in contrast, is felt by the lover deep within the soul. The lover lives with God, breathes with God, talks and interacts with God, and grows through God. At that point of yearning Him, God attaches Himself very intimately with the individual who is seeking Him. Here the individual forms a very intimate and meaningful relationship with God. God then begins to provide that purpose by providing spiritual completion and growth where God makes the devotee like Himself. He is charitable; the devotee becomes charitable. He is all-knowing; the devotee yearns knowledge. He is generous; the lover becomes generous. He is unbound and unrestricted; the lover becomes unrestricted.

Without hesitation the lover is now able to critique and evaluate. He is filled with confidence, and he is validated. He does not require any further validation. There is no fear left in him. The world is his place of journey. He will journey intellectually and emotionally, and he will grow spiritually. God is now very meaningful because He is at once the purpose and the means to that purpose. He becomes a source of liberation in contrast to the God that we worshipped previously who was a source of constriction, "Do not ask this, do not question that... do not go down that route."

The God of the lover is a very different God. He is a God that teases the hearts and minds. He is the God that intrigues us, that initiates us upon the journey. He questions us, "Look at all of these things, had it been from other than Allah would you see such consistency?" He says, "Do they not consider the Quran? Had it been from other Than Allah, they would surely have found much discrepancy."(4:82) He is open to challenge, "And if you are in doubt as to that which We have revealed to Our servant, then produce a chapter like it and call on your helpers besides Allah if you are truthful. (2:23) He says in the Quran, "Challenge Me! Bring about something better than this Quran, and if you can't, then intellectually submit that it is from a superior source."

This God is the liberating One. He rejoices in being challenged. In fact, this is a God who says to us, "I can only be attained through challenge. I can only be attained when you acquire a nature of defiance and say, I will not take anything at face value." So what if it is an observed norm for tens, hundreds or thousands of years? For so many centuries we thought the earth was the centre of the universe. There was no sacredness to that belief, but people gave it sacredness. It had to be challenged in order for us to arrive at a greater understanding of the nature of the universe. The best thing that those great men of God did was to challenge the centrality of the earth, and to break the sacredness. There was only one thing that was sacred, and that was the enquiry into the truth.

So God becomes a part of an intimate growth process where we commit ourselves fully to a life, and we begin to live a life that is purposeful and productive, in which we wholeheartedly take full stake-holding. We wholeheartedly admit that I am the one who is responsible for my own destiny. Nobody can be blamed for a pitiful end at which I arrive. There is no cousin, brother, father, mother, angel, Imam or prophet who is accountable. It my story with my God. There is no Plato, Aristotle or Socrates; in fact, Plato, Aristotle and Socrates, whom I venerate, have the same brain in their skull that me and you have. They used their minds in their journey. We need to use our minds. How did Socrates become the great Socrates? By asking and defying, by going against the norm of his time. He had to drink the goblet of poison, did he not? But he did so with conviction, he wholeheartedly sipped it down. That was his punishment and he accepted the punishment. Then you get the great Plato – the great thinker, but we see Aristotle challenging Plato at every level even though he was an intellectual giant.

Thus, God becomes a point of liberation not a point of confinement or constriction. He initiates us into a life which is a life worthy for a human being. We were created for the lofty heavens; we were not created to be earth-bound. The lofty heavens are not up above in space, rather the lofty heavens are the lofty statuses of our souls. Do we not say that the Sulayman of this world ruled over man, jinn and beasts, but the Sulayman of the heart – Husayn Ibn Ali – ruled over the Sulayman of this world? It is one thing to acknowledge God deep within ourselves and to say yes, He is a force of liberation, but then we need to ask how does He go about doing this?

I need to know what constitutes my inner liberation – my growth? I am not a solitary individual in this world. I live in a collective capacity. I live in a pluralistic context. I trade and interact. There are cultures. I have children, parents and a spouse. How am I supposed to attain this purpose in the context of my existence given that God is that deep-seated intimate factor that I bond with? We say that God has provided a religion for us, and this religion is the means for the completion of our humanity.

So, on the one hand we say that purpose is constituted by the three factors as we previously stated: intellectual completion, moral refinement, and spiritual fulfilment, thereby becoming God-like. If we take all three together, we will say that purpose is human completion, or fulfilment, but what are the practical ways in which this completion is attained through God? It is one thing to say that I am intimately connected with God, but then do I understand how my relationship ought to be with people of other faiths? How I ought to transact? How do I fulfil that purpose within the context of human life? We say that God has communicated to us a religion and this religion is the means towards attainment of that purpose through God – is that not our claim? Immediately there is an assumption in the mind that if this religion is the means of attainment of that purpose at all three levels, and if it is from God, then this religion is sacred – it is eternal. If I am following the final religion, then it is the right one and exclusively the only one. These assumptions need to be checked.

What do we understand by sacredness of religion? Sacredness of religion means that religion cannot be wrong. Then I ask a question: how much of this religion is from God and how much is from human interpretation? We say that our religion is sacred and sacredness means it is from God and therefore it is absolutely accurate. This is the meaning of "sacred", is it not? It is divine, it is holy. I will ask what is so holy about this religion? Open and study your religion and tell me which aspect of this religion has been communicated by God directly?" You will reply, "The Quran." I will then ask, "How much of your religion do you receive from the Quran directly?" You will say, "Nothing." We are all beholden to interpretations of the Quran. This interpretation of religion, how much of it is directly from God and how much is the interpretation of a human mind? You will reply, "The whole entirety of the religion in the way we have it today, excluding the text of the Quran , is human interpretation of what God is communicating." If that is the case, then one mind cannot claim supremacy or superiority over another mind in the absence of the prophetic intellect, and therefore there is no sacredness of religion at that level. Every part of this religion can be questioned. Even the clarifications provided by the blessed Prophet and his progeny are open to interpretation. Does that make sense?

The Quran, without a shred of doubt, is the word of God, but the interpretation of the Quran, is that the word of God? The answer is, no. So, the interpretation of the Quran can surely be challenged. That God given right of enquiry, thinking and critique allows us to look into religions critically as well. Much of what happens in the name of religion is just the norms of our forefathers or cultures of our community, and on occasions it is inconsistent with our sense of purpose. Before we know it these practices and beliefs that do not make any sense, and on the contrary are counter-productive and regressive, become ordained in the name of religion. If a person were to think about these things accurately, they would come to the realisation that they do not make sense. But due to sheer laziness and fear, they convince themselves that they are religious and accept practices even though they do not make sense.

I will give an example of a belief that does not add up. Your neighbour is a better human than you are in terms of being in line with purpose and Godliness. Intellectually, he knows more than you; he is open to knowledge. Morally, he is more refined than you. He does not tell a lie. He does not shout or steal. He is respectable. He looks after the other neighbours. He is charitable. He cries for the orphans of Africa, Pakistan and Afghanistan. He protests against the government for going to unjust wars. He is more refined than I could ever be. He looks beyond Christianity and he helps the Muslims as if they were Christians. He does not see religion as a form of bias against Islam. His religion and morality allow him to embrace Muslim children as if they were Christian children. Spiritually, he is far more Godly than I am. His eyes tear up at the plight of humanity. Instead of stealing he relies upon God and makes a prayer. He is not an insecure person. He has confidence. Yet I am supposed to assume, according to the Islam that I follow, that I am better than he! My heart and mind cannot make sense of this but then my religion tells me that I am better than he is, and I will convince myself that I am better. Things that can never make sense begin to make sense in the name of religion. Things that are neither productive nor fulfilling are presumed productive under the banner of "the sacredness of religion". They are presumed progressive even though they are regressive.

The Prophet came to a Nomadic society. They killed their daughters and they sacrificed their children to gods. Within no time, he transformed them into explorers and the greatest scientists, people who contributed to a new civilization. What did religion do for them? It liberated them! Intellectually they flourished; morally they became refined; spiritually they became godly. Out of today's 1.7 billion Muslims how many are of that calibre? Those previous Muslims embraced the Christians and the Jews. They treated the Zoroastrians as the people of the book. They spread Islam through their moral conduct in their interactions with others. Where are those Muslims today? Is this a sign of a "sacred" religion that is liberating people or is it a sign of regressive people under delusions of "sacredness"?

Religion has acquired the label of "sacredness" and this labelling is totally inconsistent with our purpose. So, when we say religion is sacred, this assumption itself needs to be critiqued for as soon as we say it is sacred, religion becomes untouchable. It goes beyond enquiry and we continue to cut off the limbs of thieves and the heads of people. When people say we should stone them to death, I ask where is stoning to death mentioned in the Quran? Show me one verse in the Book where it mentions stoning to death as a punishment in the code of Islam. Where does it say to burn people in the Quran? Did the Prophet not say, "If my hadith is inconsistent with the Quran, reject my hadith"?

The Quran is the communication of God. Why are the Muslims not critical? Why do they not understand things accurately? Why have they lost their God given right to have that confidence in God and to ask questions. Why has the community stagnated? Why has the religion become regressive? What is the cause of this regression and stagnation? If this is the eternal religion that the Prophet gave us, then why was it initially very productive and so unproductive today? Why are there people like ISIS who can justify their position through Islam when what they are doing is terrible and inhumane? This critique needs to be there. This open enquiry needs to be there. How can I commit myself to this sort of a religion that embarrasses me? A religion that I need to hide all the time? A religion for which I need to make excuses all the time?

I have heard preachers when they talk about religion, they have to sugar-coat things because they know it is there within the Quran , however, they have not bothered to understand the Quran . They are merely upholding those things as "eternal" and "sacred", therefore they cannot examine it openly. It is there, what ISIS are doing is all there in religion. It needs to be critiqued and re-evaluated by these preachers. They need to admit that it does not make sense at face value. I know that there is sacredness about it, there is divinity, but I do not know how. I know my God can never be such a God but I do not understand how. I need to open up my mind.

The assumption is that religion is sacred — it is eternal. So I ask, what do we mean by "sacred" and "eternal"? Let us look at religion now. Religion, by definition, is a set of teachings that give meaning and place to human individuals within the world at all levels of human existence by addressing them all. It is the broadest definition I am providing right now. In that way religion gives a purposeful meaning to life, that this is what life is all about. But this definition is a very general statement, what about the specifics? When we go into the specifics and we see that religion has essential features. Study the Quran and you will find them. What are the essential features? The essential features of religion that guarantee purpose and salvation are three: firstly, intimate bonding and connection with Allah (which the Quran calls 'īmān billah'); secondly, an eschatology and soteriology, which means the end times and *qiyāma* or the purpose towards which we are arriving; and lastly, a means to get there, which is known as righteous deeds *('amal al-ṣāliḥ)*.

These are the three essentials. These three things are not compromised in any way and are found in every religion, especially in the Abrahamic faiths. This is the reason why God grants the faithful of other religions who abide by these three essentials paradise time and again, especially in the first four or five chapters of the Quran. It says to the Christians and Jews, "You are upon nothing until you establish Torah and Injīl." (5:68) If they were so wrong in essence why would God say that? So, these are the three essential features that cannot be compromised in order for the deliverance and the salvation of a human being: the deep-seated bonding with Allah, the sense of eschatology and soteriology (that I have to get somewhere and become something, that I need to fulfil my humanity and attain salvation), and the means to achieve the first two, which is righteous deeds. These are essential and then there are the non-essentials.

What are the non-essentials? The non-essential features of religion are how the righteous deeds have been formulated. How have the righteous deeds been formulated by religion? What constitutes a righteous deed? These righteous deeds are formulated in line with the purpose, whatever is purpose-yielding constitutes a righteous deed. But it is not as simple as that because the righteous deed is contingent to the context. For instance, religion teaches us that speaking the truth constitutes a righteous deed, but in order to save the life of an innocent person from a tyrannical ruler telling a lie constitutes a righteous deed. Is this becoming clear? The righteous deed in this scenario is determined by the situation, i.e. the context. Let us give some more examples: preservation of life is a righteous deed but in order to safeguard the integrity of your community from an attacker, taking a life might constitute a righteous deed. At the level of defence, killing an opponent may constitute a righteous deed. Are you seeing that? Giving money in order to promote the cause of Allah constitutes a righteous deed, but when giving money to a Muslim state increases tyranny, withholding that funding constitutes a righteous deed. Therefore, righteous deeds are formulated in accordance with a purpose, and that purpose is the fulfilment of the individual and the collective body. So righteous deeds are formulated in differing manners, this is the non-essential part of religion. Generally, the righteousness of a deed in principle is acquired through its productivity of growth.

To recap, the essential parts of religion are: a deep-seated bonding with God to become God-like; eschatology, the responsibility for what we are becoming and the fulfilment of human existence; and righteous deeds. The aspect of righteous deeds that is to be formulated in everyday life is not sacred in its particular form. If this is clear, then we will say that in religion the "righteous deed" has two further categories. One is the permanent contributor to the righteous deed and the other is the human non-permanent factor of the righteous deed. What are the permanent ones? For Muslims, it is the *ibāda*, the forms of worship such as the daily prayers and fasting. These are the permanent features of the righteous deed for the Muslim. For instance, when you are earth-bound, pray to Allah facing the Ka'ba, when you are in space you will still pray to Him even though there is no Ka'ba. The prayer will still continue but in a different form.

Other faiths have their own permanent formulations of righteous deeds as well. How beautifully Allah says, "For all communities, We have made different ways of devotion, which they ought to observe." (22:67) You have certain rituals and ways to worship which you uphold, but Allah has made their rituals as well, which are the permanent features for them. Again, God says that all peoples have been given their direction (2:148) therefore, do not quarrel about the direction of the qibla. They have their direction and you have your direction. Those are their permanent features and these are your permanent features. Your permanent features are yielding your purpose and their permanent features are yielding their purpose. Allah says that for each people, He has given a specific Sharia and way of life *(minhāj)* (5:48).

Apart from these permanent features that give us our identity (the *ibāda*), there are certain righteous deeds that are based on the superior knowledge of God, which we have yet to uncover. These are the regulations pertaining to the consumables. God uncompromisingly says, "He has forbidden you only carrion, and blood, and the flesh of swine, and that over which any name other than God's has been invoked." (2:173) We do not know the properties due to which they are prohibited. We have yet to discover the reason, of course, we will in the due course of time. As Imam Ali ibn Abi Talib has said, "Had Allah not given you *halal* and *haram*, your intellects would have discovered it in the due course of time, but He has made you needless of it as a favour by giving it to you." So, in the area of consumables the superior knowledge of God has supplied us with what is lawful and what is unlawful. The final permanent feature of the righteous deed that God has supplied us with, in addition to *ibāda* and consumables, is the notion of "decency".

Aside from these, what else do we have in terms of religiously ordained actions and outlooks? We have capital punishment, and the notions of fair-trade. We have cultures and symbolism, and human interactions. All of these things were not introduced by religion at all! They were already present before the coming of religion. Religion merely moderated these things. There is no such thing as Islamic sociology, Islamic economy, or Islamic politics. These are human endeavours to lead a most productive, fulfilling, and purposeful life. Religion merely came to moderate them in accordance with principles of fair play and justice. So, when it is said that you cannot critique religion, I will ask what do you mean you cannot critique religion? What of religion is sacred? A social system? An economic system? A political system? None of these are sacred.

As an example, look at Islamic banking. What is Islamic banking? It does not make any sense to me. If you are talking about interest, then of course the human mind will tell you that exploiting the poor is wrong. That does not mean that interest per se is wrong; it means that exploitation is wrong! Interest can be very productive. It can be very socially-friendly. Does that mean that interest which is ethical and not exploitive is prohibited? But we are told that the text is sacred, to which I reply, yes, the text is indeed sacred but is your understanding of the text also sacred? Have you understood what the text means?

So, in religion there are features that cannot be compromised. These uncompromising features are accepted by human reason in every human community. The first fundamental feature is that there has to be a deep-seated bond with God who is the force of liberation at an intellectual, moral, and spiritual level. Nobody will disagree with this, provided that they have belief in God of course. The second essential feature is a sense of arriving at a state of completion, which is eschatology and *qiyāma*. Again, nobody will disagree with this. The final essential feature is the need for righteous deeds, which again nobody will disagree with. Apart from these three, there is nothing there that cannot be questioned. If we can arrive at that understanding of religion, then imagine how dynamic Islam becomes! If we can understand these three features and how to formulate the righteous deed outside the scope of devotion and consumables in its societal, political, and economic capacities then imagine how phenomenal religion becomes as a means towards human completion.

Imagine if the concept of religious charity was understood accurately as a means towards the growth of the community, then we would not hesitate in investing this religious charity so that it produces a greater return. In this way it would be possible to serve the community in the long term. Surely this makes more sense than keeping a segment of the community poor and just giving them handouts every time they need it. Which human mind will say that giving charity for the sake of charity is sacred because it is something ordained by God? No one will say that. Every person will say that the sacredness of charity is that it serve the needs of the community in the most adequate fashion. Every mind will agree that a beggar cannot remain a beggar. Through charity, the beggar will eventually become self-sufficient and arrive at a level of dignity where they begin to give as well. Who would disagree with this?

The label of "sacredness" is attached to much of our religion, which in turn prevents people from questioning it. On the contrary, all of it is open to questioning. So today, if ISIS say that they take Yazidi girls as slaves because it is allowed in the Quran, we will respond that the Quran had to formulate righteous deed within a given context where taking war prisoners as slaves was the norm. It modified those existing contextual norms in a moderate way in light of justice and fair-play. So the Quran formulates righteous deed in accordance with, and within the restrictions of the time. It does not mean that slavery is an eternal law of the Quran . In fact, the Quran in its own context, for the first time in history, was emancipating slaves and initiating a trend of giving back human dignity. The Quran initiated the discourse of human rights for every human being by virtue of being a human. So, the law of slavery is not sacred.

What is sacred is the righteous deed. What is not sacred is how it was formulated back in the day when Islam was revealed. With this understanding, if we look at capital punishment and cutting off the hands of the thief, we will say that the Quran formulated righteous deed in order to drive the community towards a state of godliness. There is no sacredness in cutting hands. The sacredness is to do with the purpose. Similarly, there is no sacredness in the norm of having two women witnesses in testimonials where one man would suffice. It was due to the limitation of the context. At that time women were not accustomed to retaining knowledge and so the Quran at a pragmatic level had to formulate a law to ensure the accuracy of testimonials of women within the limitations of that context.

Now what about the claims of righteousness and sacredness whereby the Shia say the Sunni are wrong because they have not understood or interpreted the Quran accurately? The mentality of we are right and they are wrong. We (Shia) smile at them whilst believing they are all dammed. The Sunni say that the Shia are the biggest agitators we have seen in the history of mankind but we have to be one with them and pray with them, however we know they are all going to hell. So, if Sunni and Shia are throwing each other into hell, what chance does the rest of humanity have of making it into paradise? This is what me and you believe because of our notion of sacredness, whereby each group says, "They haven't understood, but we have understood." This is wholly inconsistent with the message of Quran . Read the Quran with open minds. this trend is wholly inconsistent with the ethos of humanity. How can humanity ever throw a good soul into hell? How? As a human being, would you even want to belong to such a religion?

We know that the glorious Islam of the Prophet is a productive religion. It is a growth-yielding religion. It is a divine religion that can embrace humanity at large with all its differences as the Quran demonstrates. Imagine if you had been an alien who had come from a distant planet to Earth and you had to choose a religion. None of the religions would appeal to you. You would say all of them, in the name of God, are condemning and cursing each other. They all say that they love their God, that He is the Creator of all and that He is more compassionate than the mother. He loves all and He loves peace, yet in the name of that peaceful, loving and parental God they are condemning each other to the pits of hell. How inconsistent are these human beings? In reality, all of this is happening today in the name of religion!

So, the sacredness of religion is not where we think it is. The sacredness of religion belongs within the essentials: god-centricity, fulfilment and completion of humanity, and the righteous deed (that is formulated within different contexts in different ways). If we were to understand this, we would know that harmonious coexistence, mutual gain, reciprocal relationship with humanity, and appreciation of each other constitutes the essence. The slight differences are the way in which people formulate righteous deeds in accordance with differing contexts. But a righteous deed is only righteous when it yields growth and progression of humanity and godliness. A righteous deed that leads to condemnation of the other is not a righteous deed, it has nothing to do with God. It is not godly at all! Rather, it is ungodly! In fact, every feature of religion that brings arrogance within the soul is ungodly.

I will say here that the one whom we are remembering tonight may not have consider Imam Husayn as an Imam as we understand an Imam. He prayed with Husayn ibn Ali without acknowledging Imam Husayn as an *Imam*. He may have prayed with his arms folded. That did not matter to Husayn ibn Ali; it was of no consequence. It did not mean anything to him because what mattered to him was the essence of religion and godliness, not the formulation of righteous deeds in different contexts. Imagine Hadrat Hurr becomes a supreme icon for mankind! Hadrat Hurr to whom Husayn said, "Hurr your mother has named you accurately, you are a free man."

He was free and he received salvation in accordance with that essence of religion. The formulation was not restrictive for him, on the contrary, it was a means of liberation. The problem with us is that the formulation of righteous deed has become sacred even when it becomes a means of regression, and we do not want to open our minds to critique it because of our insecurity due to the claim of eternity and sacredness. That is our problem!

Night Five

In the previous lectures, we stated that there are many areas in religion where human interpretations have been taken as "sacred" despite them not contributing to the purpose of our creation. These need to be removed. The sacred components within religion are those teachings that give meaning to human life and a place within the cosmos. The sacred part of religion exists in: God-centricity, or belonging to God; eschatology, which entails a sense of real responsibility and purpose; and righteous deeds (*'amal al-ṣāliḥ*) as means for the attainment of the objective by becoming complete and virtuous human beings. How the righteous deed is interpreted and formulated is not to be considered sacred. What is essential and sacred is that deep-seated intimate relationship with God – that personal belonging. The sacred is to have this notion of responsibility that we are growing, and to attain this utmost growth. What is sacred is to perform all those actions that assist us in becoming fulfilled, wholesome, and complete human beings. What is not sacred is *how* these things that take us towards completion are formulated. Righteous deeds, as we explained earlier, are of two types: permanent and non-permanent. Neither of them are sacred. Every faith has permanent features and they are all different but Allah grants salvation to all provided that they fulfil the essential requirements.

Now that we have dealt with the assumptions pertaining to

righteous deeds, we will examine eschatology. By eschatology we mean the eventual end, where are we headed to? Where are we going? What is the destiny that awaits us on earth? Broadly speaking There are two types of destinies. One is the destiny on earth for mankind as mankind and the other is a befitting destiny that is to be arrived at on the Day of Reckoning where the human soul attains the fullness of its beauty through god-centricity. This is the ultimate sense of salvation and soteriology. For now, we will deal with the first one, the destiny of mankind on earth, although both are inextricably connected as shall become clear over the next two night since salvation is directly contingent to human destiny on earth. An accurate understanding of eschatology and soteriology determines the course that we take individually and as a collective body, our outlooks and our attitudes, our sense of right, our sense of the rights of others and our sense of piety.

Now, if we were to understand that our eschatology is based upon the fact that human beings evolve collectively and are bound by a collective destiny, then we would not be concerned about our individual wellbeing only. Rather, we would be more concerned about the wellbeing of our human community as a whole. If the final goal that is to be arrived at on the face of this earth is for humanity at large, then the course of our individual lives will be determined by the fate of the whole of humanity and consequently we will consider our success in the ambit of success of humanity in our understanding of life. For example, take a university and the individual students of that university. The success of the individual students is not only contingent upon their own personal performance rather it is as much dependent on the standards that the university sets, and the standard of the university is determined through the whole body of its students. Therefore the achievement of an individual student by and large is proportionate to the achievement of the majority of students. It is the same with humanity, in humanity's case the individual human achievement is far likely in the context of a good human society and that seems to be the natural and most befitting human eschatology.

Look at the beautiful prophets, which one of them was not a social reformer? When we read the Quran we will find that all of these prophets were committed to social reform. Each one of our Imams was committed to social reform. Apart from Prophet Yahya who sought seclusion in a cave, and maybe Prophet Khidr, the rest of the prophets mentioned in the Quran existed within communities and endeavoured to better the state of the community for that ensured their own success, that was their mission. This is what our prophets understood, that the collective bodies' success is individual success. Hence they were so committed to the betterment of the community that they could withstand their own selves being short-changed as long as it led to the betterment of the community overall. We do not find any prophet advocating an "exclusivist" faith. I say this often, Isa was not a Christian. "Christianity" came after Isa, he was much broader than Christianity. Moses in essence was not a "Jew" belonging to "Judaism". He was much broader than that. He was not an exclusivist. He was for humanity at large. Abraham was for humanity at large.

The Quran states, "We have sent you, O Muhammad, to mankind at large as a bearer of good tidings and a warner." (34:28) Prophet Muhammad was sent for mankind as a whole. Prophet Muhammad was not a prophet exclusively for the Muslims. How can he be? When he began his mission in Mecca, was there a single Muslim present when he was preaching in the vicinity of the House of God? There wasn't a single Muslim, was there? He was for mankind as a whole. Today's narrow-minded Muslim has curtailed the scope of the beautiful Prophet and his religion. Our understanding of eschatology determines how we lead our lives. For example, if we understand eschatology in a very narrow way, then we become as narrow and restrictive as our understanding of it because that is the end we strive towards. Think about this carefully.

Today we are answering the question: what is the end goal for mankind on the face of this earth? So we want to check the commonly-held assumptions regarding the destiny of mankind on this earth, which determine and affect the way we lead our lives. We want to ascertain how much of the purpose, or end goal, we are attaining and how invested we are in that purpose. So, what is the ideal destiny that awaits mankind on the face of this earth? Surprisingly, every major faith claims that there will be somebody who will come and save mankind. "The messiah will come!" The Jews believe in the Messiah, as do the Christians. The Hindus believe in the coming of an avatar. The Shias and the Sunnis believe in the coming of the Mahdi. Some believe that he has already taken birth whilst others say that he will take birth. All of these faiths believe that the destiny of mankind is that a saviour will come and deliver them. But the thing with these religious interpretations of eschatology is that they seem to be exclusivist. We say that our saviour will come to deliver us at the exclusion of you. It is a very exclusivist eschatology that only we will be the ones who will be successful, and this determines our attitude towards life.

Before we talk about eschatology from a religious point of view and the assumptions that we have, let us first try to understand eschatology within our human condition, the "existential human condition". We want to know what eschatology ought to be, in other words, what the end game ought to be for a godly human being. For a human being that God is liberating intellectually, morally, and spiritually, what ought to be a befitting eschatology? What is the goal towards which we are heading so that we can strive to achieve it? Let us examine the nature of things. When we examine any part of this world and its nature what do we find? We find that everything is on a uni-directional journey towards self-fulfilment and completion. Every seed will germinate, grow and become a fruit-bearing tree. Every conceived ovum will grow into a foetus, then a child, young adult, grown adult, moral being and spiritual being. Everything is growing – nothing is stagnant. Everything is reaching the fullness of the potential that is within it, but is this all that we are seeing? We are seeing a "collective" state of completion. We do not see only a single tree completing its journey, we find an orchard or groups of trees completing themselves. Generically, whole species are completing themselves, to the extent where the survival of each one is contingent upon the survival of all of them.

In the same way, mankind's survival has not been due to the growth and nurturing of one individual. It is where it is today due to the whole human community. Our intellectual progression, evolution, and growth is not due to the efforts and progress of an individual or even a group of people. Our knowledge, or intellectual growth, is the result of humanity's endeavour as a whole. At every point in history, different segments of humanity have been contributing to this intellectual evolution. Similarly, our moral evolution has been contingent upon different individuals and groups contributing towards moral growth, one fruit of which is the human rights declarations. So, we are seeing that it is the nature of the world and our existence that evolution and completion occur in a collective capacity. This is a feature of existence.

Existence always fulfils itself in a collective capacity, not in an individual capacity. In fact, if individuals were left on their own, nobody would evolve! Imagine if we were not in a community, we would not have a sense of art, culture, or trade. There would be no sense of morality or societal norms. These moral principles that we have is due to the fact that there are so many people interacting socially with one another. What would be the value or meaning of speaking the truth if I was the only one and there were no other people? What would be the meaning of saving a life if I was the only one? These beautiful morals only evolve because we live in a collective capacity. Do you not see that speaking the truth, fair trade, saving life, giving charity and so on are only possible in a collective capacity? So moral evolution only occurs within a collective capacity. Intellectual evolution occurs because all cultures are contributing to the sum total of man's understanding. We are now seeing that the end goal has to be one where humanity as a whole comes to utmost completion and fulfilment.

Now if a parent or a teacher sees their success in the collective growth of each individual child and student, then why should God be any different? A parent sees that their children grow far more easily together in a collective capacity, and their success and joy is when every one of their children completes themselves – attain their potential – and comes of age. Similarly, if a dean of a university or a teacher sees their success in all of their students graduating, then why should God be any different? My godliness, my sense of purpose, that deep-seated need within me, says to me that my success is in the hands of the success of humanity at large. When we look at the prophets all of them worked for humanity as a whole. Prophet Muhammad spent a lifetime in order to reform barbarians. People like you and I condemn ISIS. A person who transforms monsters such as ISIS into fine human beings is Muhammad, the Messenger. This is how he was! There was nothing but the likes of ISIS at the time when he came. He reformed them and made them into fine and upright human beings because he saw the success of humanity in a collective capacity. The Ummah that he constructed did not consist of Muslims only, rather it consisted of Muslims, Jews, and pagans together. He was so broad in his understanding that he knew humanity has to exist as humanity.

Now, there is a problem that needs resolving before we continue to examine our next assertion that humanity as humanity is diverse and pluralistic. "Religious people" may ask that how can the entirety of humanity have success when there is nothing special about humanity as a whole? This is this cancerous problem, which plagues us, that we need to resolve. We "religious people" simply do not understand the meaning of variety. We just cannot understand it. We do not understand the meaning of plurality; we just cannot understand it. This is the reason why we shout out the hadith that Islam will be divided into seventy three sects, seventy two will go to hell and one will go to heaven! If you mentioned this hadith to anyone who is critical and open, they would immediately reject it on the basis that it is inconsistent with the purpose of God. It does not make any sense! In fact, the opposite should be true. Seventy-two will go to paradise, and one might go to hell.

Do you know there is another version of this hadith that out of the seventy-three sects, seventy-two will go to paradise, and one will go to hell. That is the version of the hadith that nobody talks about because we have not been able to understand the meaning of collective destiny and plurality. We do not understand the meaning of variety. This is the reason why we say to people that you should not wash your arm in a certain direction because God will not accept your prayer. This is the reason why we say that if a person holds his arms folded during prayers or does the salaam at the end by turning his head left and right, the prayers are not accepted. If we could step out of this condition of religiosity and check this assumption, we would have a far greater prophetic understanding of what is going on.

Tell me, which two of us here look the same? Are there two people here with the same features? No, and yet are we not all the same? What joins us, what binds us? Our love for Imam Husayn. It is the same sentiment that we all share. So, there is a natural plurality here but that plurality does not cause a problem for the whole group to sit together under the banner of Husayn ibn Ali. Everyone here will claim that we are all arriving at a state of salvation through Husayn ibn Ali, and yet this gathering withstands the plurality of features, colours, genders and ethnicities does it not? When you go to Hajj you find that seventy-two, seventy-three sects of Muslims (I always say whenever there is talk about seventy-three sects that if you count the number of sects Islam has it is far greater than seventy-two or seventy-three. We believe in the hadith because we hear the hadith but nobody critically checks these things. Historically, how many sects have we had? Go and check it). In any case, at Hajj there are many different sects but you will call them all Muslims, will you not? What binds them together? It is that commonality of Hajj, the circumambulation of the House of God, the ceremonies and rituals of Hajj that are performed. Despite differences they are all called Muslims. This is something that requires understanding.

Humanity as humanity has to come to a level of success and growth, that is its end goal. So how do we resolve this? Individuality is something that inevitably produces what we see all around us all the time: variety and plurality. Look at the trees. You will see apple trees, they are all producing the same type of fruit yet they are all different trees. Look at the prophets. In Sūra al-Baqara, God says, "There is no distinction in His apostles (2:285) and on the other hand He says, 'Some of the apostles We have endowed more highly than others. Among them are those who were spoken to by God Himself, and some have been raised even higher.' (2:253)

They are different and yet they are the same. One is *kalīm* and another is *ṣafī*. One is *khalīl* and the other is *rūḥ*. One is *ḥabīb*. They are all very different and yet they are the same! There is something that binds them in essence and there are things that separate them, which are non-essential. The same truth binds them in essence making them one and what separates them is arbitrary. All of them are within the *wilāya* of God. Receiving from God and giving out glad-tidings and warnings to their people. All of them are phrasing their message differently and yet all of them are the same essentially. The difference lies in the forms that the essence is fashioned in, each brought different regulations, different methods of prayers, and yet the essence remains. All apple trees bear apples, yet each fruit is different in terms of size and colours. Then there are different species of apples, and yet they are essentially the same. This is true of every type of fruit, each is different yet they are all fruit. This is true of the whole of existence, form separates each entity in a given species yet all individuals are equal parts of that species.

As human beings, we are different in our features. Existentially, we are different. We are different in terms of our families and we are different in terms of our communities, yet at every level difference becomes diluted – can you not see this? As an individual, I am very different to every other individual but as a family I become one of many. As a family, we are very different to every other family, but as a community my family becomes one of many. As a community, we are very different to every other community, but at the level of love for Imam Husayn my community becomes one of many. As this super-community, we are very different to every other super-community, but at the level of Ummah we become one of a much greater being. Look at the way the Quran addresses the people of the Book, "Come unto that word, which we and you hold in common that we do not devote to other than Allah." (3:64) This "commonality" is that point of unity that is beyond Christianity, Judaism and Islam! Does not God say this in the Quran? And look at the broad-mindedness of the Prophet and the universality of the Quran when it addresses humanity as a whole, "We have created you from a male and a female and have made you into nations and tribes so that you may come to know that the one closest to Allah is the one most pious." (49:13) Here, Allah is doing away with Abrahamic faiths altogether! He is addressing all of mankind. Imagine, He is saying that the essence for all is godliness.

Therefore, what we are trying to convey is that individuality brings about plurality. We do not just mean physical or social plurality but more importantly we mean the deep-seated plurality of understanding God. Ask yourselves genuinely, do any two of us even worship the same God? Am I worshipping the same God that you are? Are you worshipping the same God that I am? Of course, God is the common One by name but our individual relationship with God is very different to each other. I remind you of the famous Prophetic hadith, "Salman is on the tenth level of faith, and Abu Dharr is on the ninth level of faith. Had Abu Dharr known what is in the chest of Salman, he would have said Salman is a Kafir. He would have put Salman to death. Even Salman and Abu Dharr are not worshipping the same God despite worshipping the same God.

There is nothing but variety and plurality. There is nothing but individuality and subjectivity. We are not even sitting in the same hall. All of us are sitting in the same place and all of us are relating to it very differently. I often say that if I tell you that this object is red, that is white and this is black, I cannot be sure of what you are seeing. I only see what I am seeing. We conjure up a language that is so broad in its definition of terms that we make sense with each other. When I say this is white, you do not see the "white" that I see and I do not see the "white" that you see. This is at the very simple level of mere sense perception. When I say, "The Ka'ba is so beautiful" that is a different language altogether. Beauty for you is something totally different to what beauty is for me.

There is no commonality in any of these things. Every little aspect of life is individually rooted. Plurality is a natural product of humanity – of individuality. There is nothing but individuality in this world of God, and this inevitably produces plurality. So, if there is plurality of individual beings, then there is plurality in our sense perception. Thus, there is plurality in the way in which we interact and there is plurality in the way in which we understand God. If this is clear, then know that no two Muslims are the same! No two monotheists are the same. If Khidr and Musa are the same and yet so different, then by priority no two people are the same. What binds them is their humanity, their purpose, being God-centric and evolving towards Allah.

If this is understood, then know accurately that the eventual destiny of mankind – the eschatology on the face of this earth – is that humankind becomes one family. It learns to co-exist harmoniously where there is reciprocal relationship and mutual appreciation. In fact, this "growing through each other" has always been happening anyway whether we have been conscious of it or not. The reason for this is that although there is individuality throughout existence, every individual has an inherent existential need of "the other", which results in the beautiful collective co-existence where individual entities complete themselves through others and contribute to the overall collective completion. This individual-collective relationship is so intricate that one can be forgiven for thinking that it is nothing but the collective body that exists and individuals are not of significance, or visa-verse. However, both are very real and operate hand in hand. Furthermore, collective bodies can also be viewed as distinct collectives of individuals such as nations and people of one religion, culture or ethnicity.

Individuality and collectively are always co-existing, and all individuals inevitably contribute, at different levels, to the greater collective body. For example, at one point in history the Muslims community contributed to the intellectual progression and discovery. At this point in time, the West is contributing to it. Previously, the Athenians were contributing to it before them the Egyptians– it is one family! It has always been progressive. With globalisation, which both results in and is the outcome of the sharing of cultures and migration, we are becoming more and more broader as human beings. We are becoming more and more universal. Do you not see the formation of the United Nations? Do you not see the declaration of inalienable human rights regardless of whether you are black or white, young or old, rich or poor, Muslim, Christian, theist or atheist? Do you not see how human interaction is facilitating this progression? Allah says in Quran, *"li-taʿārafū,* through interaction you will know this" 49:13

The whole of the human family has to arrive at that point of human intellectual progression, moral sophistication, and spiritual inclination of a higher order. One of the Imams had said, "If you were to know how you were created, no human would hate another one. You are all one!" I could have easily been you and you could have easily been me. I ask you a question before continuing. If me and you were born into a Christian household, what would me and you be doing right now? We would be stating emphatically that Christianity is the right faith and that everybody else is doomed or we would be trying to convert everyone to Christianity. Had we been born as Sunnis, we would have been condemning the Shias. We may not be sitting here commemorating the martyrdom of Imam Husayn.

The question is how many of us have critically evaluated our faiths? We are content with the religion that has been fed to us from the cradle. None of us have been critical about our religion. How much does this faith mean anyway? How much is it adding to the real sense of purpose? The purpose and point of religion is that it enables humanity to grow through it. A befitting eschatology is one in which humanity as a whole comes to the completion of its journey, otherwise God has failed! God says to the angels, "I will place on the earth a *khalīfa* (vicegerent)" and they replied "Will You place on the earth those who will spread bloodshed and corruption, whereas we are the ones who exhort and worship You." God answers them, "I know that which you do not know." (2:30) By admonishing the angels, God is implying that humankind does have knowledge, understands right from wrong, and has the capacity to understand Him. Here, *"khalīfa"* is not referring to one individual but to humanity at large. Adam (A.S) was not a single man. The Quran says, "Indeed, We have created *you* and then formed *you*, and then We said to the angels,

'Prostrate yourselves before Adam'. And all of them prostrated except *Iblīs*." (7:11) "You" are one being.

The success of humanity lies with the completion of humanity as a whole. Now imagine if this was the eschatology that we had in our minds, the Muslims would become the greatest contributors to human welfare. They would be the best humanitarians the world has ever seen because they also have teachings of the Quran , the Prophet and his blessed family. They would be the greatest scientists the world has seen. They would be hailed for their humanitarian efforts! They would not be producing ISIS. They would be producing fine men and women. For such people, the hadith, such as those that foretell of future technologies, would be motivations to actualize them. I often mention this example of the hadith which says that when the twelfth Imam comes you will see each other in the palm of your hands. This hadith was meant to motivate us to go and invent devices that enable this. It was not going to be a miracle. It was going to be a feat of human technology, but imagine, due to our skewed eschatology we were not the ones to invent these devices because we were waiting for a miracle. The Imam, who will bring humanity to its completion, has become the Imam who will save only us and butcher everyone else. We are exclusivists Our attitude is that I will succeed, and the rest will fail! What have these attitudes led us to?

There is a hadith that people overlook, which gives us an accurate appreciation of the eschatology that we are talking about. In "al-Ghayba" by al-Nu'mani, there is a hadith that the Imam will retrieve the Torah and the Injīl from a cave in Syria and rule over the people of Torah with Torah, the people of Injīl with Injīl and the same with the people of Quran. What does this show? That he will withstand differences! He will bring about a harmonious human coexistence withstanding the differences and not seek to convert everyone. In his system, the differences will add to a greater charm and greater growth, and how can it be otherwise? The Quran guarantees salvation to the Christians, Jews, Muslims and Sabians on the basis of belief in God and the Last Day, and righteous deeds (5:69). Thus the Prophet's Ummah consisted of Jews, Christians and pagans. Imam Ali is attributed with the statement, "If I was given the authority I would rule over the people of the Quran with their Quran, the people of the Injīl with their Injīl, the people of the Zabūr with their Zabūr, and the people of the Torah with their Torah." How can the final Imam be any different?

We have failed to understand that our success on earth and salvation in the Hereafter is contained within the arrival of humanity at the point of its glorious completion. Now look at our present eschatology, the pessimistic outlook that is ingrained in us from childhood. The earth towards the end of time will become very evil; every day will be worse than the day that precedes it and this will continue until the twelfth Imam will appear and rid the earth of injustice. What do such pre-conceived notions do to us? They fill us with pessimism and fear! We have no positive outlook towards the earth, let alone making a difference to the world. Who will want to make a difference for the betterment of mankind when you already believe that the situation is going to get worse? Who would be motivated?

Does enthusiasm and hope drive us forward or are pessimism and hopelessness the motivators of progress? Is it not hope and optimism that drives us? How inconsistent is this worldview with the way in which Allah has made us? We give the best education to our children with the hope of sending them to Cambridge and Oxford, don't we? We give them the best possible education, despite believing in this eschatology, which means we act inconsistently when it comes to our children. But when it comes to our worldview and outlook, we are very narrow-minded and pessimistic. Our attitude towards the community is that it is good for nothing. The Imam will come and deliver the community. Therefore, your task is just to sit at home on the prayer mat and become pious. What is this piety? For God's sake explain this piety to me. The "religious" people have hijacked the minds of the people by espousing this piety.

A person came to the sixth Imam and said, "I have made a solemn resolve to retreat to a cave." The Imam asked, "Why?" He said, "I have sinned when living with the community." The Imam said, "It is better to have sinned and to be with the collective body than to be alone as a hermit." He said, "But I see things that are forbidden." The Imam replied, "Even then." He said, "But I speak wrong things." The Imam replied again, "Even then." He persisted, "I hear evil things." The Imam replied, "Even then." As if he is confessing, "I commit evil crimes." The Imam replies, "Even then." Be within the collective context, you are evolving with them, and they are evolving through you!

We are filled with pessimism. What do we teach in madrasa? Everybody is evil and this world is an evil place. This world is going towards an evil end. The twelfth Imam will come and cleanse it. How strange is this? His grandfather came to the people who were submerged in evil and waiting to fall in hell! The holy Prophet did not kill them. He took them out of hell and made them into fine human beings. How can the mission of the grandson be so different from that of the grandfather? Which prophet has condemned his community outright? Every prophet, progressively, has secured more and more numbers of people. Are you are saying that the culminating glory of the prophetic trend is going to be so miserable? If this is what we teach in our madrasa, if this is the eschatology that is forced upon us, imagine what would happen if the Muslims were to rule the earth. If we believe that seventy-two sects will go into hell and that when the Mahdi comes people of other faiths will be put to death, there would be no rights for the non-Muslim at all. They would be second-class citizens. At the most the Muslims would give protection to the Christians and Jews with *jizya* (the tax paid for protection) but they would make the Hindus and Buddhists stateless altogether.

Imagine, this is our inherited eschatology!

Now imagine a world where we have a befitting eschatology, where we challenge this "exclusivity" and state that the assumption that only we will be given success and the rest will be put to death does not make sense. Then imagine how productive Muslims would become. The next head of the United Nations may be a Muslim. Not only a human being who is a fine person but as a "Muslim human being" who adds to the collective growth of humanity, who addresses the collective problems of humanity and who can go beyond his/her biases. Imagine if we believed in a positive final goal that motivated us to progress in every field. The community would get a new lease of life, have confidence in its abilities, be motivated and empowered!

The Prophet of Islam was truly amazing. The Quran describes the community he transformed as those who were on the verge of falling into the pits of hell! There were chains that tied them and weights upon their shoulders that pinned them to the ground. The blessed Prophet taught them to be moral; he freed them from the chains and shackles and he lifted the weight off them. Imagine, these nomadic tribes became a great empire and a civilisation that dwarfed the Persians and the Romans. This was due to the positive eschatology of the Prophet: you have to progress. This beautiful world is yours. Humanity is for you to contribute to.

So, eschatology is all about progression and growth, and therefore includes being bold enough to criticise our literature and religious texts that are disguised as religious but have nothing to do with religion. This eschatology is not restricted to the progression and growth of Shias or the Muslims. Your success and my success is guaranteed with the success of humanity. The end game is that through common human morals, intellectual progression, and a deep-seated sense of spirituality, human beings with their variety and plurality will learn to coexist harmoniously, appreciate one another, and gain reciprocally from each other.

That is the pedestal at which humanity needs to arrive. And the sooner we make that our objective, the sooner we begin to lead a purposeful life – a life that is worthy and in which we begin to arrive at our own success and salvation!

God envisages the human being collectively as humanity who will master their destiny and gain control over the earth and existence at large. Hence He endowed them with the capacity to learn, and He gave them knowledge of all things. In addition, by blowing His spirit into the human being, He made them all His like! Hence, a befitting eschatology is where humanity as a whole fulfils its purpose of intellectual, moral and spiritual completion, and that is the truest success that we are designed to achieve. This collective eschatology, in turn, grants salvation to the individuals of the collective by bringing them to the state of self-realisation.

Night Six

We understood destiny as two things: fate of humanity on earth and salvation in the Hereafter. We discussed the end goal for human existence upon this earth. We stated that those exclusivist assumptions, that one group of people will attain supremacy over the rest of the mankind, are wholly inaccurate, false and inconsistent with our human condition. Many faith systems have this exclusivist eschatology. We examined the verses of the Quran and the hadith literature pertaining to the fulfilment of the collective human body. Intellectually, our knowledge base increases through our individual, communal, and collective endeavours. History is composed of us all contributing in one way or another. In the Quran, God says that He taught Adam all the names. Where are these names? These names are there, yearning to be discovered – to be found. The surge of humanity towards completion is a collective endeavour. We are all evolving together. God wants us to explore! He wants us to understand. He wants us to learn. He wants us to become the supreme species on the face of this earth. He wants humanity to arrive at intellectual completion. That is the first thing.

The second thing is that humanity, as a collective body, has to become morally refined. It has to arrive at the pedestal of morality where there is agreement that humans as humans need to abide by these moral truths – these rights, whether they believe in God or not. As Husayn ibn Ali said on Ashura that, "If you neither believe in God nor are fearful of accountability in front of Him, then at least in your human capacity do not stoop to such a despicable degree. The acts that you are committing are unworthy of a human being!" There are moral values, there is something like human dignity. We also stated that morality is connected to the collective humanity. Majority of morality becomes redundant in an individual existence. Morality only has value – any sense of existence – in a collective capacity. For example, if I was the only individual on the face of this earth, speaking the truth would have no value. Being fair in transactions, being charitable, righteous, and saving life would have no meaning. Therefore, human destiny binds all of us together.

Now think about this: had we not been of different groupings, persuasions, colours and cultures, how would we explore these same human truths? For instance, if we were one tribe, one nation or one religion with the exact same thoughts there would be no notion of inalienable human rights, which is premised on difference. But due to the variety of multiplicity throughout existence, we are able to evolve to a level where we declare that there is a sense of human morality that embraces us despite our variety. And the Quran says this, "We have made you nations and tribes." (49:13)

We also touched upon the final element of the collective eschatology – spiritual fulfilment. The state of completion in which there is God centricity or belonging to God at an intimate level. Not just living a life for the sake of it, not just an arbitrary life but a real substantive life which comes through being God-centred. Then we gave the narration that when the Mahdi appears he will rule upon the people of Injīl with their Injīl, Torah with their Torah, Zabūr with their Zabūr and Quran with their Quran . God is even more explicit in the Quran that whosoever, from among the Abrahamic faiths and Sabians, believes in God, the Last Day, and does righteous deeds, they will have their reward, there shall be no fear upon them, and nor shall they grieve. The Quran is giving this message of plurality! This verse is repeated twice, and there are ample of verses giving the same meaning – from Sūra al-Baqara to al-Mā'ida. Four chapters of the Quran are stating this. The Prophet enacted this plurality in the creation of his Ummah, and the eschatology regarding the Mahdi is talking about this plurality.

To briefly recap: the collective success of humanity is foretold by our religious texts and is anticipated in light of our human condition. The final end of mankind on the face of this earth is that humanity arrives at a level of maturity despite their differences and particularities, where they see the salient truths and realise that knowledge is a common heritage that we are all growing through and adding to. In fact, this variety adds charm to knowledge. What one person can see, the other cannot because they have different perspectives, and when both the different perspectives come together the synthesis adds to the human knowledge base. This knowledge cannot grow save through particularities and differences. Similarly, common morals and common morality cannot exist save in the ambit of differences and plurality. Common spirituality, that God-centricity and becoming godly, cannot be understood save within the context of plurality.

You will see the Christian, Jew, and Muslim – Shia or Sunni and you will notice that from all of them there are people who are godly and others who are not. You will find a distinction not through religion but through another yardstick altogether: "godliness" and "godlessness". "*Lakum dīnukum wa-liya dīn.*" This is the distinction that the Quran is making, "For you is your *dīn* (religion), and for me is my *dīn*" (109:6) That *dīn* is nothing but wholesome surrender to God – the principle of all splendor and human aspirations. Only through distinctions of religion, language, culture, ethnicity and gender that we realise the all-embracing nature and beauty of the Most Beloved. Only through variety and plurality we understand that God is at once manifested through each and beyond all determinations. True

God-centricity is in transcending limitations and allowing the light of God to reveal itself through different mediums.

The Quran strikes only one distinction, "godly people" and "godless people". It is within the collective capacity that we begin to arrive at this truth, the realisation that actually spirituality goes beyond religious persuasion. You can be godly in the folds of any religion. I ask a question that if everybody on the face of this earth were to become a Muslim, would there not be differences? Of course, there would be differences. There would be differences in the way in which they understand Islam. Look at the numbers of sects we have in Islam itself. If everybody became a Sunni Muslim would there not be differences? Of course there would be differences! There would be differences in jurisprudence and theology. One will say the justice of God means this, and the other will say the justice of God means that. One will say the sunna of the Prophet means this, and the other will say the sunna of the Prophet means that.

You will never be able to rid the human community of variety and plurality. Everything is individual; there are no universals on the face of this earth. They only exist in the mind or at a metaphysical level. There is only individual! And by 'individual' we mean that there are individual existing things – you are one person, and I am one person – that is it. This individuality yields plurality. No matter how much you try, you cannot rid the world of plurality. It is not possible, and you can never do away with it.

Now, if we insist that the exclusivist position is the truthful one, that out of the seventy-three sects, seventy-two will be damned and one will be saved, then we are in effect stating that God is the biggest failure in His decision to create a *khalīfa* on the face of this earth – He has totally and miserably failed! But of course, this is inconsistent with the verse of the Quran in which God says, "Nobody will go to hell save the most wretched!" (92:14-16). It also is inconsistent with the verses that state that the

Jews, Christians, Muslims and Sabians will go to paradise so long as they believe in God and the Last Day, and perform righteous deeds. So we have a choice. Either we cling to the negative exclusivist eschatology, which is totally infested with absurdities, or we uphold the human collective eschatology, which is actually mentioned in the Quran and maintains that the overwhelming majority of humanity will arrive at that glorious state of human success.

Now, how will our acceptance of the collective eschatology shape our attitudes in this life? We will be invested in bringing about collective growth and salvation. We will be concerned with the collective fulfilment of humanity. The Muslims will no longer think in terms of their exclusivist Islam when it comes to worldly success. Rather, they will think in the terms of the inclusive state of *islam*, an *islam* that allows for all humanity and faiths to work together and collectively as one human community to arrive at that level of success destined for humanity as a whole. This concludes our discussion on eschatology in terms of humanity's destiny on earth.

Now, we move on to the other sense of destiny that is entailed in the notion of *qiyāma*, salvation in the Hereafter. *Qiyāma* is that point of individual salvation, but even here if you look at the verses of the Quran , God talks about salvation and damnation in a collective context. Sūra such as al-Maryam, al-Zumar, al-'Arāf, and many others discuss the fact that whole communities will be admitted to paradise or hell. In one Sūra, it is said that one community will curse its sister community. The latter community will ask, "Who has prepared this seat for us inside hell?" This shows that even in the Hereafter the communal identity is very dominant and that it determines our ultimate fate. The fact that whole communities have been destroyed due to their insolence and disbelief is evidence of this collective-damnation. On the other hand, notions such as "the best Ummah" is demonstrating collective-salvation, in addition to worldly success.

It stands to reason that worldly life gives communal identities to members of given communities. This identity is not only indicating the arbitrary features such as location, language, and customs. The communal identity goes well beyond these things and actually fashions the outlook of its members – the psychology, ethics, morality and spiritual orientation of the people of the communities. Thus, it is now easier for us to understand how a godly community ensures the salvation of its members due to its shared moral and spiritual orientation, whereas an ungodly community impacts its members in a contrary manner. There are many testimonials of this in the Quran where a group of people in hell lament and blame others for their ill fate.

What is the understanding of *qiyāma* and salvation that prevails through our community today? It is that my personal purity constitutes my salvation. This attitude is a huge damnation upon the community because the community believes that purification of the soul is being divorced from the world altogether and becoming pious. I ask what does piety mean for you? Is it to look miserable all day long? Is it to take the prayer beads and sit on the prayer mat all day long or to pray and fast all day long? If this is your piety then know that the Prophet of Islam said, "The sleep of a scholar *(ālim)* is better than the devotion of a ignorant person." At that time when the Prophet uttered these words we did not have the *(ālim)* that we have today – the scholars of *fiqh* and Islam. *Ālim*, at *that* time, meant somebody who was learned. Imam Ali said, "If you have a moment before death, the best thing to do in that moment is to learn something." Why? Knowledge is connected to salvation on *qiyāma*. There is something going on! It is a question of fulfilment, the completion of the human journey. How do we complete it? We complete it by becoming godlike.

I often give this example. There are certain insects, on this planet, that have soft beaks and have been created without eyes so they cannot see. The food that they feed off has to be dead insects and the only way they can feed is to dig their beaks into whatever is below them. If that which is below them is hard they will not be able to dig into it. Now consider this, because they cannot see and they have soft beaks, how are they able to live and feed? Pay careful attention as what I am about to explain is truly amazing! Through volcanic eruptions, the first level of gases that are released carry many small insects away from where they are and they die en-route because they cannot withstand the heat – so they die while being transported. They arrive at the peaks of a mountain. Before the second layer of gases are released, it snows so these dead insects are covered in snow and preserved. The second layer of gases is a stronger one so it carries these unseeing, soft-beaked insects to the mountains. They arrive and the only thing they know is to dig the surface below them. They start digging in accordance with their nature and they find dead insects there waiting for them. Imagine if a person has this understanding and then says, "Praise belongs to Allah the Lord of the worlds (*al-hamdu lillāhi rabb al-'ālamīn*)" Imagine how that person, in his or her prayer is transformed through that knowledge that Allah is so meticulously taking care of everything that exists – he begins to become godly!

This notion of "piety" of sitting on the prayer mat and becoming gloomy and miserable, and fasting all day long, what good is this piety if it does not bring goodness in the heart towards the other? What good is such piety if it does not bring reformation of character and soul? As Rumi gestures, "Why don't you understand? Goodness is not in *ṣalāh*. Goodness is what you become through that *ṣalāh*." If after that prostration you are not surrendering to Allah then what value was that prostration? If after that hunger of the fast you are not becoming charitable towards the other, then what good was that fast? If after going around the Ka'ba seven times your heart does not become one with the Ummah of the Prophet Muhammad then what good was that circumambulation around the Ka'ba? This notion of "piety" that we have today is a bit of a failure! We all ought to be pious, so we can attain salvation. However, salvation is not attained through this sense of piety. Rather, salvation is attained through the fulfilment of our human growth at an intellectual, moral, and that deep-seated spiritual level.

People often say this to me after hearing my speeches you know what, the non-Muslims are definitely going to go to hell. My response is why are you so obsessed? Paradise is so big that if all seven billion of us go to heaven, it will still be infinite and endless! What is your problem? Why can't you stand others going into paradise? You can't even stand each other going into paradise! What is wrong with you people? Your God is giving paradise to all people – He is the charitable one. Why have you become such misers, and that too in the name of God?

Think about what I am saying. I know it might seem a little comical but think about it thoroughly. You know something, when I sit with a Christian I say you may have a truth that I might need. If you convince me of anything, I will take it. I am in a state of surrender to my God. This formalistic Islam, Christianity and Buddhism mean nothing to me – these are merely titles. That which is true is what God is giving and my task is to receive it from wherever I receive it. It belongs to me, and we need to share as human beings. When people say that non-Muslims are going to hell, I respond well how many Muslims are going to heaven? According to you, seventy-two sects are going to go to hell as well. It is going to be a very lonely place this paradise of yours! And for you to a have a heart like this, despite your neighbours being godly, shows that you have already kindled a hell inside your soul! You are in the process of making your own hell and heaven right now, in every moment of your life. You are the hell and you are the heaven.

I will give this example, somebody asked me, "What is success and what is failure?" I said, "You are the yardstick of success and you are yardstick of failure." When a student goes to university and he asks what is failure, I will not say failure is getting less than a desired mark on the paper. Rather, failure is when you don't study and fail to actualize knowledge. What is success? I will not say the hundred-thousand-pound job you land after your degree. Rather, success is you arriving at that state of competency. *You* are the failure or *you* are the success. So, if you can condemn someone to burn in hell despite them being god-centric then it shows that you have kindled your own fire. Why would any soul want to condemn another to hell? Are we better than the prophets? Find me one prophet who when asked about the people of earlier times said they are all in hell. The prophets said that we don't know; Allah knows best.

The Prophet of Islam said I don't even know what will be done to me and you. I don't even know my own fate, let alone the fate of others. I am at the mercy of my God. How can I pass judgment upon others? Which Quran are we reading? Why are we reading without thinking, without understanding? This level of arrogance! This level of ungodliness from people who are worshipping God five times a day? Look at the Muslim community killing each other and tearing each other apart. It is due to these false assumptions, which need to be checked, evaluated and critiqued. The Quran needs to be read once again.

When somebody says to me but they don't believe in Prophet Muhammad! I will say did God know this or not? If God is saying that the Sabians, Christians and Jews are going into Paradise, does God know that they don't believe in Prophet Muhammad or not? God does know it yet we are baffled. So I will say as a response where in the Quran has God given centrality to the belief in any prophet? Where? Where has God said to believe in the Prophet in order to arrive at salvation? The Quran has always said to believe in God and the Last Day and do righteous deeds, you will have your reward. You are your point of growth and the prophets are intermediaries.

Where in the Quran has any verse given centrality to the

prophets? The Quran says, "Verily, in the apostle of God you have a good example"(33:21), and "If you love God, follow me; God will love you and forgive your sins." (3:31) It starts with you and God, and it ends with you and God. I do not deny the intercession of the prophets, saints and Imams . All of them are valid. But the main point is always the centrality of God and the individual, and the growth in the individual. So, it is possible for a person who does not believe in the Prophet Muhammad to nonetheless believe in, and live in accordance with, the essence of Prophet Muhammad's teaching. That individual may not perform the daily prayers, circle the Ka'ba, or keep fasts in Ramadan like us and yet have salvation through their own system of devotion. Look at this verse of the Quran, "Every community faces a direction of their own, towards which He turns them ... So compete with one another in doing good works. (2:148) Therefore, it is Allah who decides the different rites and rituals for different communities.

The meaning conveyed by the aforementioned verse and it's like is that you have your rituals and Sharia, and they have their rituals and Sharia. Don't worry or argue about them, instead compete over goodness. Now, does the "religious-other" believe that lying is good? Do they believe killing is good? Do they believe their God ordains them to indecency? Do they believe their God ordains them to lying and cheating? No! So, they are believing in, and practicing, the principles and essence of Prophet Muhammad's teachings. They may be practicing the "forms" of Moses but the "essence" of those forms is the same as Prophet Muhammad's. They are seeing the Prophet Muhammad in a different face but they are believing in the same essence.

The ultimate destiny, or the ultimate *qiyāma*, is a point of salvation. It is for those who become godly. It is the completion of the human being or a soul through embracing God totally. And this salvation is only possible through growing through God and removing our lack through God. "I am scared, I am frightened"

– convert this into confidence and trust through reliance on God. This is salvation on the Day of *qiyāma*. "I am ignorant, I cannot understand the glory of my God." Gain knowledge and try to find God in everything. "I am morally deficient. I distinguish in terms of colour." Then go beyond colour. "I distinguish in terms of gender." Then go beyond gender. "I distinguish in terms of religion." Then go beyond religion. "I distinguish in terms of social status." Then go beyond status. These are your deficiencies. *Qiyāma*, or salvation, means that you reconcile these frailties in a state of godliness.

Surrender to God in your individual capacity so that you become godly. Give away your frailties and surrender to God. In return, God bestows godliness upon you, that is salvation for you and it is available for one and all. Imagine if a person arrives at that level of understanding of salvation, that salvation is not something that will happen on the Day of *qiyāma* when God takes out a book and says I am going balance your good deeds against your bad deeds. Rather, God will say you are the book today – read yourself. In Sūra al-Kahf, al-Isrā and other places, it is implied that you are sufficient as a witness on yourself on this Day. (17:14) And that your skin will speak on that Day. Does He not say that? *You* are the yardstick of success and failure. That is it.

There are no books that are going to be read in the way we imagine. God does not need witnesses in the realest sense; you are the witness. You are in a process of becoming. Use this time in the world productively. It is a place of great opportunity. Every instance is an opportunity for you to give yourself away to God and become godlike. Go and learn, explore nature, see the secrets of God. How beautifully the Prophet said, "O Lord, show me things as they are! Let me understand You to a level of greater depth." How amazing is the Prophet of Islam. At the conquest of Mecca he stated that "No man has a claim over another man – all of you are equal." Look at what he is implying, there is no free man higher than a slave. You are all at the same pedestal of humanity.

Thus, you are in a state of becoming. This is what the Prophet has taught us. Every moment should be spent profitably. Every moment should be seen as an opportunity. The biggest and greatest favour God does for us is to allow us to break our intellectual idols. Do you know what intellectual idols do to us? They bring us to a state of stagnation which leads to damnation. There is no restriction in God! The only restriction is in the heads of the followers. "I can't do this! I can't ask this! This is my limited worldview!" Imagine, if we became free men and women completely, and understood the purpose of life and the world for what it is. We would break the shackles, evolve and became complete.

A beautiful story comes to mind. Moses was going to the mountain on an occasion and he was met by a disbeliever who said, "Moses, where are you going?" Moses replied, "To the mountain." The disbeliever asked, "Shall you engage with the Lord in speech?" Moses answered, "Indeed." The disbeliever said, "Ask Him, it is His claim, is it not, that He is the One who sustains all?" Moses said, "Indeed." The disbeliever exclaimed, "Tell Him that I do not believe in Him, so He should hold back His sustenance from me. And if the air that I breathe is from Him, tell Him to take it away and snatch it from my mouth!" So, Moses engages with God. And God says, "Moses, give him My response. Tell him that, "Your Lord bids you peace and He says to you that you can be My creature and reject faith in Me but I, being your God and Lord, will never stop sustaining you for as long as I keep you alive."

That state of godliness is where you and I belong. We need to arrive at that level. How beautiful and pertinent is the story of salvation as recounted by certain orators that when Prophet Muhammad was told by Allah, "Do not stand at the graves of the hypocrites and do not seek forgiveness for them. Even if you ask seventy times, I will not forgive them." The Prophet said "If only God had told me to stand there and seek forgiveness seventy times whereby He would forgive them. I would have stood at every one of their graves and sought forgiveness for them." Do you know how godly Muhammad, the Messenger of God, was? He told his companions, "Gabriel came to me last night. He said, Muhammad, God gives you the option of forgiving half of your Ummah on the Day of *qiyāma*." The companions were taken aback, they were scared and asked, "O Messenger, what did you do?" He said, "I refused." They breathed a sigh of relief. Then Gabriel came back and said to the Prophet, "Muhammad, God gives you the right to intercede for all of your Ummah." The Prophet smiled and said, "I will take that. I will intercede for each and every soul within my Ummah and will ensure I take them to Paradise."

That is the level of godliness at which we need to arrive. We need to be busy in learning, contributing to humanity and becoming godlike. We need to be busy in forgiving and sharing whatever we have. As the fourth Imam said, "If somebody swears at me, O Lord, allow me the patience to not swear back. Allow me to pray for him." A level beyond even this is the following prayer of an Imam, "O Lord! If he is right then forgive me and if he is wrong then forgo his faults." In the story of salvation and final destiny, God has informed us of things for which we have made a pact with Him. One is that He will give us opportunities to grow towards Him. These opportunities are challenges. He challenges us at every point and these challenges are opportunities for us to grow towards Him. When you hear a contrary opinion to the one you are used to, that is an opportunity. It is a challenge to the mind. It is an opportunity to go to a stage beyond the uninformed opinions we hold.

The Muslim community should be the most liberated community when it comes to entertaining intellectual challenges, not the one that cries, "Bar him! Ban him! Don't read this or that!" No, this is not what the Muslim community is supposed to be. Islam means surrender – to surrender wholeheartedly, intellectually, morally and spiritually. How can a person grow if their minds are not challenged and their assumptions are not questioned? Does the Quran not challenge this attitude, "When they are told follow what God has revealed some answer, 'Nay, we shall follow that which we found our forefathers believing in and doing.' Why, even if their forefathers did not use their reason at all, and were devoid of all guidance?" (2:170)

In addition to the intellectual challenge, the other challenge from God is the moral challenge. Here, we have to go beyond our biases and acknowledge there is commonality of humanity between us. Arbitrary distinctions such as race and gender are of no consequence at all. At times, a parent comes and tells me that thier daughter wants to marry someone outside the community. I respond so what, if he is a good man, let her marry. Just because he is not from your clan, or whatever superior race and culture that you think you are is not an acceptable reason to refuse his proposal. Most of these people who are suffering from this superiority complex have taken birth inside their superior cultures and races, have they not? What a beautiful poem attributed to Imam Ali, "Be the son of whomever you want, but be righteous. The praise that comes to you by being righteous will make you needless of any lineage." This is a moral challenge, "This person is different to me in terms of status." Try and let go of your biases. This is the ultimate goal: to evolve and grow.

At times, God challenges us at the core of our beings in a way that causes suffering – and this reality, suffering, is intertwined in the fabric of our existence! Suffering gives the greatest opportunity for us to grow through. Suffering is not pain or loss. It is a result of our interaction with that pain or loss at a psychological level. When God takes away somebody from us it causes suffering. When God snatches our wealth or social status from us, or when He brings enemies in front of us, there is suffering. But in truth, that enemy is an opportunity for us to grow through. The enemy is a friend for you to grow through, for you to love that enemy, for you to forgive, for you to embrace. It is an opportunity to grow and evolve. Why do we not understand that life is too short? It has not been given to us to hate people or to form the sort of attachments with them that ruin us. It is a life of opportunities.

Suffering is an integral part of human existence. A person is not supposed to scream and shout in despair or break. They are supposed to grow through suffering. When my ship is surrounded by stormy waters, there is no need for me to become bewildered. I should stay calm and say O Lord, if not through these stormy waters, then through a little clot in my blood can You take me. Who can stop You my Lord? You do not need to be dramatic in order to kill me. My Lord, let me find You in the roaring waves. Let me find You in the pitch darkness of the night. Let me embrace You, O Lord. You are my light amidst darkness! You are my security in the stormy waters!

That is the opportunity that awaits us. When a limb is cut, say O Lord, it belongs to You and it has returned to You. When danger is in front us say *la ḥawla wa lā quwwata illā billah*, there is no strength and there is no might but through You.

This is how suffering is supposed to drive our evolution. The more the heart suffers, the more refined it is supposed to become. The more we witness the death of dear ones, the more the attachment with God is supposed to grow. The more the wealth is snatched away from us, the more needless we become through God. How beautiful Husayn is when he says, "O Lord, the One who has formed me in the womb of my mother, creation after creation in three layers of darkness. And You brought me into this world so proper and complete." How beautifully he gestures, "O Lord, before You brought me into this world, You ensured that the sun rose, that the benevolent heavens showered upon us, and that the earth produced. Before You brought me into this world, You ensured that sustenance awaited me in the bosom of my mother. Before the teeth arrived and the need arose, You ensured my sustenance was waiting for me at the table. O the One who has taken care of me so properly in the days that have gone. Shall You not take care of me in the days that are to come!?"

So, when all of my business empires crumble, it is an opportunity for me to find that wealth which is undiminishing. Foolish are the souls that crumble under pressure. Godly are the souls that grow under pressure. Failed are the souls that become inhumane because of their enemies. Successful are the souls that grow in humanity and godliness through their enemies. How the Muslims become complacent! They thought that they are the Muslims so they can never lose and will always be guaranteed victory. But they lost at the battle of Uhud! The Quran informs that there are things that God will give and take. Yesterday was a victory for you and today is a victory for your enemy, so what is the big deal? Sūra al-Āl Imrān informs us that your success is to find God through both victory and defeat. The defeat in which you find God does not constitute a failure – it is the greatest form of success for you. God is saying both worldly victory and defeat do not constitute success and failure with Me. What constitutes success and failure is what is happening inside you. If there is a victory and you become complacent and so arrogant about it that you lose Me, then you have failed.

Do we not say that Husayn won the war and the battle? But he was cut into pieces, how has he won? He arrived at the fullness of his potential, and the sword upon him contributed to his great success. Through his suffering, he becomes a refined and beautiful soul. The way in which he has been described! The enemy had not seen a man so hungry, thirsty, brutally oppressed and wounded. There was no strength left in him, fallen and yet his face radiated. There was a serenity about his being. His lips moved in the eulogy of God. How he evolves through human suffering!

Every religion, in principle, has sought to create godly communities through their respective teachings in order to guarantee the salvation of the maximum possible number of its adherents. The great prophets understood well that the ultimate aim of God was the deliverance of humanity as a whole, and that the eventual salvation was inextricably connected to the creation of a successful godly-community on earth that ensured salvation of the people in the Hereafter. The whole struggle of Imam Husayn was to bring about the rectification of the affairs of the Ummah. As he stated, "I have not risen in order to create discord; rather, to rectify the affairs of the Ummah of my grandfather. I wish to ordain to good and dissuade from evil." This rectification and creation of a worthy community on earth was fundamentally due to the aim of bringing human beings to the fullness of their existence which in turn ensures the eventual salvation for the majority.

Night Seven

Last night, in the context of salvation we discussed opportunities, challenges, and sufferings whereby a human individual is awakened to God. This is the great beauty of God that we alluded to. He relates to me very personally. There is this belonging to God, a very intimate belonging to God, through which I am becoming godlike. I am casting aside my inhibitions, restrictions, fears, and anxieties; and they are changing into confidence, security, and a state of liberation. He is liberating me through Himself at every point and this is the deep-seated purpose I find within myself. We also discussed that my purpose and success is contingent to the purpose and success of everybody else. So my success is the success of my community. Mankind as mankind has to succeed before I can succeed. We said that the end game on the Day of *qiyāma* is how godly I have become myself; however, this too is largely in the context of the salvation of humanity as a whole. We discussed individuality in existence – everything is individual. This yields subjectivity, which then results in plurality.

Now we move onto another issue. Our fundamental assumption is that God has spoken to us in the form of revelation – the Quran, which is the Book of God. The Quran, in todays' world, is used to justify every ideology. Anyone with any preference or outlook will be able to justify it through the Quran. Even ISIS root their monstrous behaviour on their understanding of the

Quran. An Islamic system will derive the legitimacy of its form of governance from the Quran, whether it is a Shia system or a Sunni system. We read the Quran, at times, in order to legitimise our own selves or our own inclinations and our own predetermined outlooks or mind-sets. On the one hand, the Quran is supposed to be a revelation from God, and on the other, certain verses cause embarrassment to its followers. When certain verses are mentioned about beating wives or giving half of a share of your inheritance to a woman (even in social setting where she is a provider and a carer), we find that it becomes a point of great struggle. We have to ask what are our assumptions of the Book of God?

If we were to become very critical of our assumptions regarding the Book of God then this Book may lead us to a more accurate path. God says, "It is He who shapes you in the wombs as He wills. There is no deity save Him." (3:6) God has created me, and the Prophet has said, "He fashions you in His image." God does not have a face, so the image of God is something far more profound, it is His nature. Our nature and goal in this world is to be purpose-oriented. That purpose is the fulfilment of our humanity. It is to evolve, grow, and arrive at the fullness of our human potential. Now, how can His word be inconsistent with the nature with which He has created us? If God has reflected Himself in us then how can He command us to that which in inconsistent with that nature? How can He endow His *khalīfa* with one nature, and say something that is totally different to it within the revelation?

We are now coming to the crux of the issue. There is no doubt that the Quran is the Book of God; it is His revelation. Now we jump to the naïve assumption that the Quran is eternal. It is meant for all times, till the Day of *qiyāma*. We have this assumption that it has everything inside it. Is it not a belief in our theology? God says, "There is nothing wet or dry but it is recorded in the clear book." (6:59) The Muslim feels that whatever He has said is to be taken literally. But there is no mention of kangaroos in the Quran, and yet the belief that everything is in the Book of God entails that kangaroos must be in the Quran. Find me a verse that talks about kangaroos. Look at these naïve assumptions: it is eternal in its literal meaning and it has every single thing inside it and is value-based.

If we are being honest, one thousand four hundred and thirty eight years after revelation, we find that certain parts of the revelation do not bear value. They are inconsistent with human rights, for instance, the practice of slavery is outlawed and "beating women" has no place in the modern world. Yet, these examples, according to the assumption of the eternality of the Quran , are supposed to be for all times and places. I ask you when some verses of the Quran are inconsistent with human morals, how do we address this issue? The problem with the community is that it assumes things and does not critically evaluate them. Everybody wants to believe that the Quran is eternal, and that it has everything inside it but nobody wants to check these assumptions. The other problem is that nobody reads the Quran for the sake of understanding it. How inconsistent is this community?

The Quran says, "Verily, this Quran guides to that which is just and right" (17:9) and "Let there be no doubt, it is a guidance for all the God-conscious." (2:2) The narrations say that when things become ambiguous or appear dark as a darkened night, resort to the Quran for it will guide you. It will provide the light through which you can walk. How much does the community use the Quran to directly access guidance? The Prophet said, "Compare my hadith against the Quran; if any of my hadith are inconsistent with the Quran throw them away."

There is a verse in the Quran that states, "If it was from other than God, you would find many contradictions." (4:82) Now, has anybody read the Quran to see whether there are discrepancies? We already have a preconceived belief that there are no discrepancies. Imagine if a person were to analyse the Quran to see whether there were any discrepancies, how much more they would be guided by the Quran? The Quran says, "Will they not, then, ponder over this Quran or are there locks upon their hearts?" (47:24) How many of us say O God, Your Quran is supposed to be eternal and all-inclusive, but I really do not understand how beating a woman is consistent with human ethos? Does anybody ask, O Lord, why should two female witnesses be equivalent to one male witness? It does not make any sense! There are women here from Oxford and Cambridge; they are graduates of the highest institutions of learning. They are not like the women of Arabia who used to forget. They are able to retain information accurately. This is highly inconsistent and it is due to this assumption that we cannot question the word of God. We need to unravel this assumption.

First, let us give a brief prelude to this discussion. God mentions the word "*islam*" and its derivatives in the Quran . The word is used in the context of prophet Ibrahim. Can that be the same Islam that you and I are following as an "organised formal religion"? It can't be, can it? God questions the Jews and Christians that why do you call Abraham a Jew or a Christian when Judaism and Christianity came after Abraham? He lived and died prior to these formalised religions. This Islam, the foramlised, organised one, has come after Ibrahim. So, Ibrahim was not this type of Muslim like us. Isa, Yaqub and his children were all *muslims*, but what type of *muslims* were they? Not this type like us. When we look at these verses, as Allamah Tabatabai states in his commentary, we will conclude that there is only one *dīn* with Allah that He calls "Islam" meaning surrender and submission. In this one *dīn*, not in terms of our formal Islam, Ibrahim was a Muslim, Musa was a Muslim, Yaqub was a Muslim and Muhammad was a Muslim. Therefore, when God says, "the *dīn* with God is Islam" (3:19) He means that the *dīn* – the way of life – is the Godly-life. The way of God is Islam It is a way of life that is totally God-centred. It is stating the essence of the one true *dīn,* "surrendering to God" without its formalistic features.

Returning to the discussion about the eternality of the Quran, see that there is a distinction between the "Quran" (the revealed text) and the "Book". The "Book" is mentioned in the Quran as "*kitāb*" and "*dālik al-kitāb,* that Book". The revelations of Sūra al-Baqara occurred to the blessed Prophet in Medina. It is the first major Sūra to be revealed was in Medina with all its regulations, societal rules, contracts, and forms of devotions. Here the verse starts, "*dālik al-kitab,* that Book". I am asking you, does "that Book" refer to the Quran as in the revealed text that we have? Look at the Quran very accurately and read it. God says in Sūra al-Wāqi'a, "Behold, it is a noble Quran in a hidden Book, which none can touch save the pure of heart." (56:77-79).

In other places, God states We gave Isa the Book, We gave Musa the Book, We gave Muhammad the Book. What is the Book? When we look critically and analyse all these verses, it becomes very clear that the Book is the reality of all realities and this Book has been revealed in the form of the Torah, Injīl and Quran. That is the reason why God says that the Book it is being revealed to the prophets. Once we understand this we come to this phenomenal realisation that the Quran is eternal in its essence, but in its formulation it is bound by its context. Therefore, all of the sacred scriptures, whether it is the Torah, Injīl or Zabūr, consist of the same eternal truths that we were talking about in the previous lectures.

None of the sacred texts will say that lying is good. None of them say that killing is good! God states in Sūra al-Mā'ida:

> *And convey to them, setting forth the truth, the story of the two sons of Adam - how each offered a sacrifice, and it was accepted from one of them whereas it was not accepted from the other. And Cain said, 'I will surely slay you!' Abel replied, 'Behold, God accepts only from those who are conscious of Him'. But the other's passion drove him to slay his brother... Because*

of this We ordained unto the children of Israel that if anyone slays a human being, unless it be in recompense for murder or for spreading corruption on earth, it shall be as though he had slain all mankind. Whereas, if anyone saves a life, it shall be as though he had saved the lives of all mankind. (5:27-32)

You can see that although it was revealed to the Israelites, it was intended for all of us to learn from that revelation. All of these books, in essence, are saying the same thing. They are talking about human morals: be righteous, give life, transact properly, do not kill anybody, and so on.

There was a Medinan man who had heard that there was a sorcerer in Mecca, and that people must not listen to this sorcerer's words because they bewitch the listener. When chapter of the Cattle was being revealed in Mecca he was present, and He narrates, "I went to Mecca and saw Muhammad standing with a group of people and talking. He was reciting the following verses: 'O people, Do not kill your children. When you transact, transact fairly. Do not sacrifice your children, We are sustaining you and We will sustain them. Do not lie. Be just and righteous. When you make an oath, fulfil it. Be good to your parents." That man said, "My goodness! He is talking about human values and the social ills that have dragged our community to its destruction." Those verses, if you search, are also in the Torah and Injīl and within human morality as a whole. The same essence was contained within the teachings of Musa and Isa. The same revelation! What was different? There is something that is different among the revelations to the prophets, which is secondary. However, the essence comprises these morals, god-centricity, spirituality, and the deep-seated purpose and meaning through God.

Look at Christianity, it talks about becoming god-like. Look at Judaism and its mysticism, it talks about becoming god-like. The ultimate goal for all of humanity is when the human being begins to reflect her/his Creator. When one becomes as charitable as God, as loving as God, as giving as God, and as forgiving as

God. When one arrives at a state of preferring the "other" over oneself, becoming complete through God, leaving insecurity and becoming secure, leaving fear and becoming confident and liberated. Every scripture teaches the same thing. So, at the level of morality and spirituality, every scripture is preaching the same thing because they are reflections of the same "Book", the same truth, the same reality!

We believe that every successive Sharia replaced the one before it, right? So, the Sharia of Isa modified and rectified the Sharia of Musa. Now, Isa only said one thing, "I have come to make many things permissible for you that you have prohibited for yourselves." Isa did not come to say that lying is good or being an enemy of God is good. Did he teach that? Were those things abrogated from the teachings of Moses? Isa said that whatever Moses said is right. Moses said saving life is good, being charitable is good, being god-centric is the only purpose. So, what did Isa change? When Prophet Muhammad came, did he change any of the essence of morality and spirituality that Musa, Isa, and Abraham taught? Did he say anything inconsistent from the time of Adam? When Cain killed Abel, God said that it was wrong. Did the blessed Prophet Muhammad say that it was right? Did Ibrahim, Nuh, Musa, Isa or anyone else say that it was right? I hope this clarifies that "the Book" has been supplying its eternal features to every revelation and that "the Book", which is the eternal Book, is revealing itself in every era with slight differences. What are these differences? It is formulating itself differently in accordance with the different levels of progression of mankind.

At the time of Musa, the Israelites were coming out of captivity, in accordance with that limited context, the essence and social morals were fashioned as "do" and "do not". In the time of Isa, those same morals acquired a greater sophistication in their formulation, which is known as "the context". In the case of Prophet Muhammad, the context was a bigger human community, or a broader humanity, which included the interaction of various faiths within humanity. He observed that the godly and the godless people existed within every faith and they were all living and interacting together. So, in his revelation, the same essence was formulated slightly differently. What was the purpose of the revelation? The purpose was to give people the inclination to acquire knowledge, become morally sophisticated, and become spiritually rooted with God. That is the purpose and essence provided by the Quran. So, the eternal aspect of the Quran is the essence. What is not eternal about the Quran is the way in which it has formulated that essence.

Our attitude, when we read the Quran, should be to try and understand the Quran as a revelation that has come in its own context. The context of the revelation was the socio-political situation of the Prophet and the challenges that he faced. Hence, the reason why the Quran is in the language spoken by the Arabs of his time. The entirety of the Prophet's surroundings constitute the immediate context in which the Quran came and formulated itself. That is, the eternal truth formulated itself within that limited context. So, when you say every word is eternal, I will ask you about verses that have been abrogated. One verse of the Quran that commands not to go to see the Prophet without giving charity was abrogated after Imam Ali gave this charity. How is that verse eternal?

Therefore, the Quran is eternal in its essence; it is temporal (non-eternal) in its formulation. In the formulation, the context plays a vital part. For instance, the adopted son of the Prophet, Zayd, is mentioned in the Quran. The name Zayd has no value to you and I today. There is no eternity about the name Zayd, but it had to be mentioned because he was the immediate context for that revelation. What is eternal is the meaning the verse is trying to convey through the example of Zayd. But "Zayd" is referring to a person with that name, how is that eternal? If we understand the Quran in this way, then we will definitely admit that the universality of the Quran lies in its eternal message and not in a particular formulation. Therefore, whenever we read the Quran we must have an attitude that it needs to be read in its proper context.

To recap: the hidden Book reflects itself as the different revelations of God throughout history in accordance with the context of each specific revelation. Thus, "the Book" expresses itself as the Torah in a given context. The Book expresses itself in the form of Injīl in the context of Isa. The Book expresses itself in the form of Quran in a given context. It is the same Book refashioning itself in different forms. Religion, or *dīn* – the one, eternal way of life with God, expresses itself in "forms" of Judaism, Christianity, Zoroastrianism, and our formalistic Islam. It is the same truth being revealed again and again! It is the same salient Godly truth. One *dīn* and one Book, formulated in different ways. It is like you explaining mathematics to a nursery child, then you explain maths to a child in primary education, and then to somebody in the secondary level of education. The essence is the same but the formulation has changed. It is the same truth but it has changed from level to level to level.

Now, people often get startled when I ask about abrogation in the Quran. Everyone believes in abrogation, that verses were revealed to our Prophet that cancelled out other verses which were previously revealed. For example, in Sūra al-Baqara God says, "We do not abrogate a verse or cause it to be forgotten but that We bring in its place one better than it or its like." (2:106) Or consider the following verse from Sūra al-Baqara that is abrogating an implied law:

> *It is lawful for you to go unto your wives during the night preceding the day's fast: they are as a garment for you, and you are as a garment for them. God is aware that you were deceiving yourselves, and so He has turned unto you in His mercy and removed this hardship from you. Now, you may lie with them skin to skin, and avail yourselves of that which God has*

ordained for you, and eat and drink until you can discern the white streak of dawn against the blackness of night, and then resume fasting until nightfall; but do not lie with them skin to skin when you are about to abide in meditation in houses of worship. These are the bounds set by God. (2:187)

Previously, the regulation in the month of Ramadan was to abstain from sexual relations for the entire month. However, God knew that the people were disloyal to themselves and continued to have intimate relations during the month of fasting, so He abrogated that law, allowing such relations after the fasting hours. Here the question is: how can abrogation occur if the Quranic law is eternal? Why does Quran ic law abrogate its own self? Why do we have verses that abrogate other verses? Our assumption is that every verse is eternal, but one verse has cancelled another verse, so what does it mean? It means that the abrogated verse has been cancelled in its entirety, so it is no longer active. But if it is not active, how is it eternal? It is eternal in its esoteric meaning. It is eternal in its essence not in its formulation. Thus, the Quran is eternal in its *essence*, not in its *form* – the formulation is contextual.

We are obsessed with the laws of the Quran, which are only contained in approximately five hundred verses out of the total of six thousand three hundred and forty eight odd verses. For example, why is the inheritance of women, in this day and age, half the share of the inheritance of men? If she is earning, providing and caring, then why? The context for the verse of inheritance was that the woman was the carer and the man was the provider. Whatever inheritance a woman received at that time would go towards her personal savings because she would be provided for financially in any case. Today, in this part of the world, women are not being provided for because they are the provider and carer simultaneously. Thus, it does not make sense that she should get half the share of inheritance in today's context in these countries! It is a *legitimate* question that can be asked. Furthermore, it is not confronting any "sacred" belief of the Quran. As we stated in the previous lecture there is nothing sacred. "Sacred" is only the search for the truth. Our enquiry for the truth is sacred; nothing else is sacred. God encourages us on the quest for truth.

Now, you may ask that why did Isa come with a different Sharia to Musa? The answer is that the community had evolved. So, why did Prophet Muhammad come with the Quran and modify the Sharia of Isa? Because the community had evolved. Now, I am asking you that today, after one thousand four hundred years, has the community evolved or not? Five hundred years after Isa, Prophet Muhammad modified the Sharia of Isa. Bear in mind that the modification was not in essence, morality, or spirituality, not in terms of purpose but in terms of formulation. I am asking you that after one thousand four hundred years, has nothing changed? The only thing that is being challenged here is the notion of the "eternal" formulation of those eternal beautiful truths. That is *not* a challenge to the Quran, it is a challenge to the naïve interpretations of the Muslim minds! It is nothing else. It is not something to be startled about; it is quite an obvious question that everybody should be asking.

Let us look at the situation of The English Defence League (EDL). When soldiers were coming back from Afghanistan, a group of Muslims were condemning and cursing them, and the English people were horrified. Their reaction was to condemn Islam as a whole. Now, look at the situation. The English people felt that these poor soldiers – our sons – went to liberate Afghanistan from the Taliban, so they were doing a favour to the Muslims. Now, when they are returning after being injured and killed in Afghanistan, the Muslims are condemning them to hell. This situation is understandable from their perspective, it is right? On the other hand, the Muslims are saying but you had no right to go to Afghanistan. You killed our brothers over there! Thus, they are condemning and cursing them. The Muslims also have a right.

If only both groups could go beyond their own perspectives, if both could just see the situation from a pictorial perspective – a holistic understanding – they would recognise that they are both right and wrong. Both sides have some truth and both sides have something wrong. If people from both groups could acquire a position of neutrality and look at themselves and the "other" and say I can appreciate your perspective, and I can appreciate our perspective as well. So, all of this animosity led the EDL to question the Quran. They said look at this Quran, it is such a barbaric book! We asked them how is it barbaric? Is it barbaric in its God-centrality? No. Is it barbaric in its human morals and virtues that it talks about? No. So, how is it barbaric? Their problem is in the way it talks about such draconian forms of punishments and the rights of women etc. It is primitive in that sense. I ask you that if we were not Muslims how would we have seen the situation?

Let me give you another example, I visited India and on the day of my arrival, the Hindu people, who had a special festival, were going to the mandir to worship. I said *subḥānallah*, may God bless them for their sincerity and the truth that they have in their hearts and guide them to a greater truth. But then they started singing their *bhajans* (prayers) from early morning till evening, and that became too much. The next day it happened again. For six days this continued, and I thought enough now. Anyway, I went back after a few months and it was happening again. Now, me, not being a Hindu, was able to say that this is a waste of time. This is truly a waste of time. The point is that had I not been a Muslim, perhaps I would have been able to make judgments about those things that Muslims are doing that are not right, which perhaps the Muslim cannot make? Just as the Hindus could not see that what they were doing was a waste of time. They could not see that pouring milk over a stone was wasteful. I could see it because I had no emotional attachment but they could not see because they were emotionally invested.

We need to ask ourselves: am I so emotionally invested within my Islam and my assumptions that I cannot see the truth for what it is? Maybe we need somebody from outside to tell us that look this is how I see your religion. Muharram does not mean suspending two months of normal life. It does not. Where does it say that for two months you cannot transact, buy, sell, or marry? I am referring to the sub-continental cultures because the Arabs, Iranians, etc. don't have this. We, from the sub-continent, can't buy, sell, or wear proper clothes. It's all black and then there is *ma'tam* (beating of the chest), *marsia* (eulogy), green and black flags, and more. Where does it say that for two whole months we have to be consumed in all of this? Anybody looking from outside will say this doesn't seem right. Husayn ibn Ali was a great man, he is supposed to prompt intellectual progression, moral sophistication, and spiritual attachment to God. Think about these things very carefully. This is a sensitive topic, which is why I am taking time to go through it.

Now, if we look at the content of the Quran, it is theological, historical, cosmological, and metaphysical. It has philosophical arguments; it has beautiful mysticism, esoterism, sociology and politics. It has stories of the prophets containing beautiful morals and human virtues. Hence, it is eternal because it contains the essential truths of "the Book" of existence. If that is realised and if we can open up and read the Quran for what it is worth, then, by God, the Quran is an uncorrupted guide that will lead us. It will enlighten our hearts! It will not be something restrictive, regressive or counterproductive. It will be something that gives us evolution and growth. So, as opposed to opening the Quran and reading it in Ramadan for the sake of reward, a person will be reading the Quran in line with its purpose: to give knowledge, refine morality, and establish that deep-seated relationship with God.

Who after reading the Quranic verse, "If My servants ask about Me tell him, I am near. I respond to the call of he who calls, whenever he calls unto Me" (2:186) would not become confident in God? Who, after reading this verse, would not become empowered spiritually? Which sinner would not become hopeful after reading, "O servants of Mine who have transgressed against your own selves, despair not of God's mercy. Behold, God forgives all sins." (39:53) Who would not become confident, when God says, "O man! What is it that lures you away from your noble charitable bountiful Sustainer?" (82:6) The hearts begin to move! How wonderfully God is explaining the wonders and secrets of creation in the Quran. It prompts the mind to think. This is how the Quran can add to that beautiful purpose within us, as opposed to becoming a stumbling block for the Muslim community by adding to their rigidity.

I have made this point before. All those Muslim preachers who when they are asked about controversial laws in the Quran (that were meant to be contextual) who react by emphatically denying that they have any place in Islam, are sugar-coating the truth. You can ask any one of them, "Do you believe slavery is an eternal law? They will respond, "It is in the Quran." So then I ask, "Why do you lie to the press? Admit that you believe in something that is inconsistent. Or say that you have not understood the Quran because it cannot ordain anything that is contrary to the standard of human morality. Admit that you have not understood it instead of being hypocritical – believing in one thing, and saying another." In fact, slavery was a contextual necessity of the time that they had to take slaves. However, the Quran initiated the trend of emancipating the slaves.

Another big disservice to the Quran is the belief that *thawāb* (reward) is procured simply by reading the Quran in Arabic, or in Ramadan, without understanding it. How can anyone gain reward if they do not understand it or if their knowledge-base has not increased? How can anyone gain reward in the truest meaning if they do not become better morally, or if they do not become grounded spiritually? What is *thawāb*? Is *thawāb* a little candy that God gives to you on the Day of *qiyāma* for being a good boy? Seriously, is this what reward is? God states in the Quran that this is the reward that you have earned yourself. This is the fire that you have prepared for yourself. If you read the Quran accurately, it says that you are the author of paradise and hell. This is your fire that you have made and this is your reward that you have earned. Whatever you became inside yourself in the life of the world, you are now seeing outside in this life of the Hereafter. Reward is growth through the Quran. Sin is merely regression.

I give this example, which I have repeated many times, the Quran was revealed to the blessed Prophet and through it he was able to rescue a community that was on the verge of falling into the pits of hell. He was able to rescue a beast-like, monstrous community from its ultimate destruction and bring it to the lofty status of humanity. But many Muslim preachers read the same Quran, and through their narrow understanding of it condemn the majority of the Muslim Ummah to damnation. Is this a problem with the Quran or is it a problem with the attitude of the reader? The same Quran that delivered humanity is being used to condemn humanity. If the Quranic assumptions can be critiqued and evaluated without fear, then we can open up that beautiful truth that is within the message of the Quran, which will lead us aright and give us the growth that is so required from within.

Imagine how Godly the Prophet and his family were through the Quran itself. Husayn ibn Ali, on Ashura, raises the Quran and says, "O people, I call you to arbitration through this Quran. O people, ever since I understood right from wrong I have never lied in making any claims." He is using the Quran in that fundamental manner. That Quran has added to his spiritual being and made him of that prophetic substance!

Night Eight

Yesterday we spoke about the Quran and questioned the basic assumptions that we make regarding its nature. We discussed how cultures pre-exist every Revelation. The Prophet introduced Islam in a particular time and place that had its own cultures and practices. The Islam that he introduced was not at the exclusion of the cultures that existed. It fitted into those cultures. There were certain cultures that were barbaric, so inhumane, that he banned them. Others he modified. Some he reformed. Thus, these contexts need to be understood accurately. He initiated many reforms within the limitations of his context. However, because of the contextual limitations it was not possible for him to conclude the reforms. For example, he initiated the whole discourse on human rights and the rights of women, but he could not possibly conclude them since issues such as "rights" are evolutionary and context-dependent. As humanity is constantly evolving and growing, our contexts (social and cultural) are constantly changing and therefore, "rights" will change as well. Thus, he could not have concluded the discussion on human rights. He merely initiated them within the restrictions of his own setting. So, the Quran needs to be read with that contextual limitation in mind.

Before we proceed into today's lecture, we need to recap some important points. We said that the Quran, in essence, contains eternal spiritual and moral truths. It encourages us to think and understand. It talks about the salient human morals that are inalienable and the spiritual connection with God. But, at the same time, the Quran had to fashion these moral and spiritual teachings with befitting forms in a particular setting of the time and place of the revelation. The context of the revelation and the era of the blessed Prophet with its societal and cultural norms, its language and knowledge base generally were a limiting factor that determined how the divine teachings were delivered and the forms they acquired. So, when we read the Quran, we need to bear in mind that it was revealed fourteen hundred years ago and appreciate its content within its own context. Therefore, the eternity of the Quran is contained in its spiritual and moral teachings that are fashioned around the society of the Prophet.

Let us clarify this further. You will see that the Quran is talking about the immediate situation of the Prophet. It is mentioning his challenges, the psychological state of the Prophet, and what was happening to the Prophet. It is to an extent Prophet centric – that is, it centres itself upon the Prophet's situation. Thus, the Quran mentions the wives of the Prophet and his blessed family, and the wars that the Prophet is fighting. Now, within these contexts, the Quran gives us its eternal truths that go beyond those situations and events that were regulated by the revelation.

The Quran, as is the case with all other revelations, has to be very pragmatic. 'Pragmatic' means that it has to be an immediate source of guidance for the community it addresses. It cannot give eternal truths without formulating them, without giving them a structure in the form of individual and societal laws. Why? Because people in general do not have the sophistication to be able to formulate these eternal truths for their particular context or daily life. So, God, through His Grace, does that for the community of the faithful.

For example, the Quran states that when it comes to bearing witness if you cannot find two men, then one man and two women will suffice. The reason for requiring two women is that if the woman who is testifying were to forget then the second woman can remind her. Here, this law is formulated in accordance with the limitation of the immediate context – that women were unable to retain information accurately. But at the same time, it is supplying the eternal truth, which is the importance of accurate testimonials. Today in the West we employ the same principle when it comes to people with learning disabilities. They are required to be accompanied by another person for support when bearing witness in court, in case they forget.

Therefore, when we read the Quran we need to bear the context in mind. When we keep the context in mind, we immediately begin to understand that the eternity of the Quran is not restricted to the particular formulation provided by the Quran at the time. This leads us to the fundamental question that if the formulations of the essence can change then what is the meaning of the Muslim identity? We typically think of our identity in terms of the forms, or the laws, of Islam that we adhere to. But if we agree to this distinction between the essence and the formulations and we agree that we need to reinvestigate the Quranic laws, then what happens to the Islamic identity? What distinguishes a Muslim from a non-Muslim? If we were now to re-think all the laws (*aḥkām*) of Islam or reinterpret them in accordance with today's context then where does that leave a Muslim in this world? If we realise that laws are context oriented and can be refashioned in our own framework, what exactly is it that makes an individual a Muslim?

There is a distinction to be made between laws that are known as "devotions" (*'ibādāt*) and "transactions or interactions" (*mu'āmalāt*). The devotional acts were novel; they were introduced by the Prophet, but the rules of transactions were merely modified by the Prophet in accordance with the principles of justice and spirituality. Based on this distinction of laws, it is clear that the identity of a Muslim, as the Quran states, stems from the ceremonies of devotion: Hajj, prayers, fasting, etc. Of course, the language of the Muslims such as *inshāllah*, *māshāllah*, *salām 'alaykum*, *astaghfirullah*, etc. also contributes to the identity of the Muslim. Therefore, Muslim identity forms due to the specific God-centric language and the devotions in Islam. It is not formed by the regulations governing transactions and interactions. They have nothing to do with Muslim identity *at all*.

So, when we engage with the questions of the rights of women, children or slaves and we try to establish the truth through sophisticated analysis of the text, this in principle, has got nothing to do with Islam directly. The identity of Islam is specific to the devotions only. So long as the devotions are maintained, the Ummah identity exists, as does the Muslim identity. But this Muslim identity, as envisaged by the blessed Prophet, is supposed to be so broad that it does not maintain any exclusivism. The Quran exhorts the people of the Book who have their own specific rituals and devotional ceremonies to unite with the Muslims within the ambit of the Unity of God.

Going further, how about the Shia identity? Surely, if we reform Islam to such a degree, then we will lose our Shia-ness? Look, the Shia identity is due to the acknowledgement of the *wilāya* (authority) of the Prophet and the Imams, and to acknowledge that the Imams were the best and noblest guides after the Prophet due to their prophetic nature. That means acknowledging their deep-seated spirituality and saintliness, their connection with God and being God-centric. This is what causes a person to be a Shia. The Shia identity is not defined by the category of *mu'āmalāt* at all. In fact, it is not determined by either folding your arms or keeping your arms open during prayers. Rather, the Shia identity is determined by the deep-seated sense of Godliness and spirituality that comes about by emulating the God-centricity of the Prophet and his family. So, remember, the Muslim gets his or her identity from the *'ibādāt* of Islam. Thus, when we read the Quran , we must read it with this background in mind. We must always keep in mind that the eternal truths were formulated within the context that the Prophet found himself in and therefore that limited context does not constitute the eternal aspect of Islam. The ethos of morality and spirituality that it conveys is the essence, and thus it is eternal. Everything else is subject to evolution and growth.

Ask yourself, have we not evolved today? According to the literature talking about the period of the twelfth Imam, people in a futuristic world will be able to move through thought. So, I am here right now and I will be able to transport myself to Australia within the blinking of an eye, according to the religious literature. Now, if I can transport myself to Australia within a few seconds would I be considered to be a "traveller" for the purposes of shortening the prayers or being exempt from fasting? Of course not! The "travel" that the Prophet was referring to entails hardship and fatigue, and it was due to the hardship and fatigue that God gave the charity of halving the prayer and breaking the fast. If through thought alone I can be in Australia, where is the fatigue? There is no fatigue.

The modern transactions that we have today and things such as the stock markets have no precedence in Islam. We do not have to take this situation back to one thousand four hundred years ago to try and make sense of it within the context of the Prophet. The Prophet's context did not know this level of transaction. It is a new world altogether. The principle of fairness, that the blessed Prophet applied to the norms of transacting is one of the essential factors in determining what is socially acceptable and productive. Such principles will direct our minds to understand whether these contracts are valid or not. If they are not, then the salient principles will guide us as to how to modify them so that they become valid. Things are always evolving and changing. Technological innovation are and will continue to impact all of us – our lifestyles, outlooks, sense of rights, etc. Every single facet of life will be affected in one way or another. Nothing will remain intact. So, the *'ibādāt* will remain the same by and large with some fluctuations, but the *mu'āmalāt* cannot remain the same!

Moving on, one of the points we will discuss today is relativity. I need to take you through this issue from the Quranic perspective. In this world of ours, every community is growing at different levels, and so, what is valid in one place may not be valid in another place. There is relativity. There may be women physically maturing in certain regions of the earth at an age that is different to other regions. Also within the same region despite the age of physical maturity women may acquire psychological or mental maturity much later than their physical maturity. What would be the implication of this? The responsibility of such women in regions where they mature more quickly is greater than those women who do not mature as quickly. "Responsibilities" and "rights" are contingent upon our existential level. Rights and responsibilities go hand in hand. As we are able to bear responsibilities, so we are afforded rights. But every region matures differently and that is why we have different systems in different settings. In some regions women may mature at the age of thirteen; but in other regions, at the age of fifteen or sixteen. Similarly, different rights and responsibilities become effective at differing levels of maturity within the same region. For example, responsibilities and rights that are contingent upon a certain level of mental aptitude will only apply after that level of psychological ability is arrived at despite there being physical maturity in the same women. Here, the Sharia will address these subjects differently from region to region and in a gradational manner within the same region.

However, even with these elements of relativity, it does not mean that we do not have universal standards. There are universal standards, some of which are not to be compromised or applied gradationally as far as possible. But for the most part within the universal standards there is a contextual application, which inevitably makes them relative. We see this from region to region, do we not? For example, many modern world countries value the right of its citizens to self-determination, but in the UK the right to vote is postulated at the age of eighteen whereas in other regions it may be at a younger or an older age. We see different rights and responsibilities afforded at different ages. This shows that there are different levels of competency at different ages existentially. These are adopted in a particular region communally because everyone in that region shares the same lifestyle, and therefore, people normally mature physically, psychologically and intellectually – more or less – at them same time. So, although some people in the UK may be competent enough to vote before the age of eighteen, the law is still set at eighteen based on the deemed competency of the majority. The point is that there will be a natural relativity from region to region so that different regulations apply to different regions. Notice, the eternal value in all of this is growth whether in the worldly sense or becoming virtuous and God-centric. However, the application of the eternal value will vary from region to region and from era to era. With this being the case we cannot have one standard taken from the sacred text and applied across the board equally and for all times since capacities are existential and contingent on varying contexts.

Let us come back to the essence of the Quran. When we read the Quran we find a monotheistic message. God is very clear that this is the only message the Quran is exhorting in a variety of ways. It is trying to liberate us! It is trying to take us to God and make us extremely God-centric. As human beings, we are very private individuals; we are very insecure and frightened. We are almost veiled and concealed. We are actually concealed to our own selves; we do not even know our own selves. We lead a life of pretence. We are extremely pretentious! What the Quran does is that it slowly and gradually unveils us. It takes us on a beautiful journey. It replaces insecurity, frailty and lack, with confidence, courage and completion. The message of the Quran is a monotheistic message. God wants us to complete our journey by finding Him and replacing our inadequacies with His beautiful completion!

God asks us to acknowledge that He is the only God. Unfortunately, the Muslim stops at that formal acknowledgement. In fact, the acknowledgement of a Muslim, for the most part, is actually based on their culture, religious education and upbringing. A Muslim fails to take the personal journey in the acknowledgement of God. But that is exactly what the Quran tries to do – it takes us on the journey. The Quran says look at this world! When you read the verses of the Quran, it prompts us to think. At every point, God tells us a story and then suddenly He exhorts look at the heavens! Look at the earth! Look at the rising sun! Look at the moon! Look at the birds! Look at the tides!" At every point, it draws our attention back to nature. Observe nature – see how meticulously it is designed. Through this thinking process, God is opening our minds. He tells us of other people who observe the earth and suddenly they exclaim, "O Lord, You have not created any of this in vain!" (3:91)

So, there is a purpose in all of this creation. God wants us to take that journey prompted by the Quran to reflect upon His creation and to understand that there is a meticulous level of consistency. Everything is happening for a particular reason and all things are intertwined so beautifully. Allah is inviting us to think. Imagine, He is asking us to ponder. Can all this be from two authorities? Can these be isolated events? Don't you think that there is a purpose here? Don't you think that there is a unity that prevails over all this multiplicity? Don't you think that you need to comprehend that beautiful unity that embraces all this variety that you see? Read the Quran with the attitude that you are on your journey to find the truth and to find Him, and it will open your mind.

The Quran also rids us of all our anxieties and distractions.

God often addresses the Meccans, "Why do you claim that one must enter from the back of the house? Enter from the front of the house." (2:189) The implication is that there is no merit in all these cultures that you have invented and concocted in the name of God. Again, God addresses the Meccans in Sūra al-An'ām, "You say this is prohibited and this is permitted – These are your fabrications!" (6:143-145) He says, "The foolish people will say, 'What has turned them from the qibla which they formerly observed?' Say, to Allah belong the East and the West." (2:142) There is no value in which direction you face. There is no value in these distractions, ceremonies and practices. See beyond it to the Unity of God. Find your God deep from within yourself! You will see that all these practices, ceremonies and rituals are meaningless. They are merely distracting you. They are taking you away from your goal.

I ask the Muslim community why are you are killing each other over your rituals and ceremonies? This obsession with your own rituals and the other's rituals has been reprimanded by God in the Quran. At one point, the "pious" and "righteous" people claim superiority on the basis of facing their holy directions in the East and the West. God responds:

> *True piety does not consist in turning your faces towards the east or the west, but the truly pious is he who believes in God, and the Last Day, and the angels, and revelation, and the prophets; and spends his substance - however much he himself may cherish it - upon his near ones, and the orphans, and the needy, and the wayfarer, and the beggars, and for the freeing of human beings from bondage; and is constant in prayer, and renders the purifying dues; and the truly pious are they who keep their promises whenever they promise, and are patient in misfortune and hardship and in time of peril: it is they that have proved themselves true, and it is they who are conscious of God. (2:177)*

Goodness is believing in Allah, believing in His messengers and His Books, doing good to others, establishing prayers and giving zakat. These are the good deeds. God *wants* moral righteousness and spiritual focus. All these other things are means of distractions.

Look at how wonderfully God liberates us and brings us to the monotheistic message. He says I give life and I take life. I give sustenance, and I withhold sustenance. I give fame and dignity, I take it away. Your job is not to be concerned with any of these things! You are not supposed to be worried with the fear of death. I will give death and when I give death nothing can stop it. He says:

> *Wherever you may be, death will overtake you - even if you are in towers raised high. Yet, when a good thing happens to them, some people say, 'This is from God,' whereas when evil befalls them, they say, 'This is from you, O fellowman!' Say, 'All is from God.' (4:78)*

Even the great Sulayman is not offered respite to sit down and he is taken standing up. Why should I be afraid of death? Why should the fear of death rid me of my peace of mind? Why should the greed of this world and sustenance rid me of my noble principles of godliness and moral righteousness? Why should I cheat anybody for the sake of my sustenance when God is saying you will not get more than what I have destined for you. Imagine how it liberates! Why should the fear of death make me bow in front of un-godly leaders? Why?

Look at the incident of Qadhi Shurayh, when Ubaydullah ibn Ziyad summoned him in order to get the death warrant of Husayn. The Qadhi replied, "How can I? He is the grandson of the Prophet!" Ubaydullah ibn Ziyad threw a sack of gold. The Qadhi exclaimed, "Do you bribe me with money!?" Ubaydullah ibn Ziyad throws another one. The Qadhi responded, "Indeed I am old." He throws another one. The Qadhi said, "I have young children." He throws another one. The Qadhi decided, "Indeed, the hadith of the Prophet states that an outlaw must be put to death." Amazing, is it not!? How long did Qadhi Shurayh live for after that?

Look at the story of Umar ibn Sa'ad. Imam Husayn said to him, "Will you go to war to with me?" Umar replied, "But the land of Ray has been promised to me." Imam Husayn offered, "I will give you the river that Muawiya tried to purchase from us. We did not give it to him, but we will give it to you." Umar ibn Sa'ad said, "The land of Ray is close to my heart." Do you know what Imam Husayn said to him? "You will not get a fistful of the wheat of Ray." Mockingly, Umar ibn Sa'ad replied, "A fistful of barley is sufficient for me." It is narrated that all night long Umar ibn Sa'ad contemplated, and expressed his thoughts in the form of poetry: "Shall I kill Husayn and become worthy of the yokes and eternal fire? Shall I spare Husayn and abandon the land of Rey? The land of Rey is the apple of my eyes, and they say God is most forgiving indeed! I shall put Husayn to death, repent for two years, and rejoice with my land for the rest of my life." Think about it, Umar ibn Sa'ad never received Ray! If he had understood that what is destined for him will come to him anyway, would he have been persuaded to commit that crime?

Should I lose my sleep at night over the worry of the morning – a morning that I am not even sure will come? Or should I sleep peacefully at night, being with my God? If I stay awake, should it not be with my Lord, thinking of Him and worshipping Him? Look at how God liberates us in the Quran. He says that life and death are in My hands. Your sustenance is in My hands. You don't need to lie. You don't need to cheat. You don't need to waste your sleep. You don't need to become sleepless at night worrying about the morning. Your glory is in My hands. Your disgrace and humility are in My hands. I know what I am doing. Your task is to find Me! That is what He teaches in the Quran – do not be distracted by any of these things. Find Me! If I place somebody in front of you who is challenging your whole belief system, then I have done that deliberately.

He works at the psychological level and starts liberating us there. Then there comes a point where He says there is no intermediary between Me and you – end of story. It is you, it is I! You will all come to Me individually, one by one. In this world of yours, there is nobody for you but Me. Nobody has any authority. Nobody has any intercession. Nobody can be an intermediary save by My consent and My grace. Your job is to be focused on Me. Become a monotheist. Away with all the distractions. Open up and give yourself to Me in utmost surrender! Therefore, the message of the Quran is a Godly message. It is absolutely God-centric and yet it is in sync with our nature. He understands that you have the need in your nature for symbolism, so have symbols. They are also valid but only to the extent that they bring you to Him, not to the degree that they distract you. If we seek help through others they can only assist us if He allows it, otherwise they have no authority.

Thus, the monotheistic vision needs to be accurate for that is how the Quran liberates. On an intellectual level, it says think, and fulfil your purpose. At an emotional level, God says I know your insecurities and fears. I know you are gripped with fear. I give life, death and sustenance. I give friends and enemies. Leave that all to Me! Find Me through all of that! And then, at the level of worship God says how dare you put anybody between Me and you? He says call me, and I will answer, does He not? When the Meccan pagans were told to be monotheistic, they said, "Well, we don't worship these idols. They are only things to take us closer to God." Do you know what God said in response? "How dare they do shirk? Have I ordained these things for them? Tear them apart and come to Me." Look at how beautifully the souls of the prophets, Ali ibn Abi Talib, Hasan and Husayn yielded to God. How wonderfully they went to God.

God assures us in the Quran, "I have destined everything

for you before I created the heavens and the earth, so that you may not rejoice at anything that comes to you and you may not frown at anything that leaves you. Your task is to come to Me through all these trials." At the same time He says I can change whatever I want. How amazing is this! On the one hand, He says if something is taken from you, thank Me because I have destined it. I have destined it for a particular purpose. On the other hand, He says if you are afraid of destiny, know that I can overpower it. Do not submit to it. Stand in the face of it and try to change it. How wonderful is this? How wonderfully it empowers us. Do not feel defeated at any instance, but at the same time, when you have done your best accept God's decree.

When we read the Quran, we see that God introduces Himself to us at two levels. One is at a very intimate and personal level, and the other is as that formal God. From the formal aspect, He is Allah the Majestic and the Sustainer of the worlds. "He is the Originator of the heavens and the earth. There is none like Him. He alone is the all-hearing, the all-seeing." (42:11) The personal God is the One we implore from deep within our hearts, "*Yā Rabbī* – My Lord!" Here, God is "my God" at that personal, intimate level. It is in a very personal capacity that I know Him where there is no pretence because He knows me better than I know myself. At this personal level, I can implore God and stand in front of Him as and how I am.

Have you ever been on an airplane and it becomes turbulent? We lose all formality do we not? We lose all pretence. We say O Lord, O Allah, in that state of panic and in that state of desperation the personal God, who we have an intimate connection with, responds. What happens in the mosque when we are in relative safety and comfort? We only find the formal God, we do not find God at that personal level. But we need to know God at both of these levels. On the one hand, we know Him as the God of the worlds; there is nothing like Him – the Lofty and the Majestic! At the same time He is intimately with you at that level of subjectivity and individuality.

Both of these beautiful aspects of His are present in the Quran – the Transcendent and the Intimately Near. He says you are My creation. You don't need to pretend with Me. Be yourself. When have I ever pretended with you? I have accepted you for whoever you are with all your frailties. Even if you are hiding from yourself, don't hide from Me. Open up to Me. I am that deep intimate friend of yours who will not judge you, who will accept you as you are. And when we are able to do this, to open ourselves up, this is when we begin to form that deep-seated connection with God. The Quran is the most beautiful book which liberates. If we could only read it accurately, imagine the type of people we would be! It empowers us and gives us confidence!

Night Nine

We have arrived at the final deliberations in this series where we will talk about the grand being of the blessed Prophet Muhammad. The Quran says, "You have a prime example in the being of Muhammad *rasūl Allah* (Messenger of God) if you wish to attain God and the Final Day." (33:21) This verse states that in terms of attaining the purpose the example of Prophet Muhammad is integral. Why? Because our purpose is to find God who liberates us at an intellectual level, refines us in our morality, and gives us that deep sense of meaning in this life. He gives worth to this life. He becomes the direction of our lives. He becomes the means towards that direction. He is the utmost fulfilment of our human journey! Now, in order to attain our purpose we need to wholly surrender to God so that God can cultivate and nurture us. He will mould us and bring us to the completion of our existence.

In fact, God is the purpose in its entirety because He is nothing but knowledge, he is devoid of any ignorance. He has no insecurity or lack within Him and hence God has the finest of morals. He is the purpose; in truth, God is our purpose. It is in this context that He says in order to attain Him and the Last Day, where the Last Day is an expression of completion and fulfilment of the human journey, you have a prime example in Muhammad, the Messenger of God. If you follow the blessed Prophet, his example will teach you how to attain salvation in the fullest sense whereby you become a godly soul and mirror the beauty of God.

I ask the Muslim community what does Prophet Muhammad mean to you and me? To be quite honest with you, in the Shia community Muhammad *rasūl Allah* is almost non-existent. I think we need to be brutally honest about this. People get offended if instead of *"rasūl Allah"* I say "Muhammad" or if I fail to say ṣallallāhu 'alayhi wa ālihi wa sallam – May the peace and blessings of God be with him and his progeny. But I call him "Muhammad" through utmost love. The protocols that we impose and that are instilled in us have made Prophet Muhammad so formalistic that the essence of blessed Prophet is lost altogether. There is no relationship with Prophet Muhammad in the deepest sense. It is only a formalistic relationship.

Now, how many of us know about his prime example? Apart from the peripheral aspects of his life such as his date of birth and death, how many of us know about his utterances or statements? How many of us know of his conduct? How many of us are aware of his integrity? His example is an integral part of our salvation! Although he is not an "essential" feature of salvation, as we stated previously, Allah has made him "integral" to the attainment of salvation, just as the other prophets are integral. Their example needs to be understood accurately and then emulated.

What example of Prophet Muhammad is the community following? He has become the most superficial part of the setup of our communities. When we go to Hajj, I often say, to the displeasure of many, when you are lecturing on the roof of the Ka'ba, why do you not talk about Prophet Muhammad? Where is the example of Muhammad, the Messenger of Allah? If you talk about the blessed Prophet on the roof of the Ka'ba, the non-Shia who are listening to you will say these people are endowed with the example of Prophet Muhammad. As opposed to them saying there is everything in these talks except for the Quran and the Messenger. These two important aspects are always missing.

What is our assumption of Prophet Muhammad? It is that

he is the best of God's creatures. I ask how is he the best of God's creatures? Tell me! Does anybody know anything about him? Let us evaluate this and then I will expand on the meaning of "the best of God's creatures". Was Prophet Muhammad born inside the Ka'ba or was somebody else born there? Was he better than Imam Ali or not? But he did not take birth inside the Ka'ba, so how is he the best of creation? Did Prophet Muhammad speak when he was in the cradle? No, but Isa did! Is the blessed Prophet grander than Isa? How is he better? He does not take birth inside the Ka'ba nor does he speak in the cradle, so how is he better? Do you understand what is going on? We have begun to look at things so superficially. There is no understanding of what this glorious individual is all about. We have become a faith of miracles, superstitious beliefs and empty claims.

The orators always recite that when Imam Ali ibn Abi Talib took birth inside the Ka'ba, the Prophet went inside and held him. Then Imam Ali said to the Prophet, "O Messenger of God, What shall I recite for you: the Torah, Injīl, Zabūr or Quran?" This is what we hear from the pulpit. God said to the Prophet in Sūra Yūsuf, "You did not know the stories before My revelation" so, how did Imam Ali know the revelation ten years before the Prophet? Be open-minded because something has gone terribly wrong. We need to understand this and we need to put things right. Now, if Prophet Muhammad heard Imam Ali speaking inside his cradle would he not have said, "*Subḥānallah*! He is like Isa." But we do not find this in the authentic narrations of merits of Imam Ali ibn Ai Talib. We have become so superficial. There is no example of the Prophet left at all. He is only there as a cosmetic feature for us to feel good but his example is not present within the community – it is nowhere to be found! No one studies Prophet Muhammad.

Take the example of Prophet Isa, he spoke inside his cradle and he was conceived without a father. Now, can anybody emulate Isa? According to popular narrations, he did not marry. We marry and have children. We have heartaches and trials in life. Isa did not have them to the same level, did he? He was grand and lofty but he did not have the trials of life that me and you have? Hence, the two billion people that follow Isa – actually worship Isa, how can they emulate him? There is no doubt that he was "love" and this is why so many are devoted to him. However, unless we admit that at times Isa felt anxiety, hopelessness, sense of failure and sin from within, then how can Isa be a role model? A role model, or a prime example, is somebody who I can relate to.

Now, the Prophet Muhammad is the finest example ever produced for mankind. He does not split the seas in two. He does not cast a staff that becomes a serpent. He is not thrown into a fire that becomes a rose garden. He does not breathe life into the dead. He does not speak inside his cradle. And yet, he is the best of people, the most superior human being to have ever walked on the face of this earth. I am not saying this blindly and neither is Muslim theology making empty claims! Even the orientalists are beginning to say that Prophet Muhammad was the finest example of a human being, and the most successful one at that. Where is his success? Where is the beauty of this man? It is in his humanness – at the core of his humanity.

The Quran is his miracle and example – not a snake, nor splitting the sea in two, nor resurrecting the dead, nor anything of that sort. His degree of human completion was due to the revelation from God! As Lady Ayesha says, "The Quran was Prophet Muhammad's mentor." The Quran nurtured the morality of the Messenger of Allah. Prophet Muhammad is the product of the revelation. What makes him so profound is that he had every weakness and human challenge that me and you have but he was able to reconcile that frailty, weakness, and humanness within the lofty ranks of godliness. Prophet Muhammad came to a pedestal where he did not even need angel Gabriel. He was that lofty – and yet still totally human! This is what makes him the example par excellence – a *real* role-model. None of the prophets before him went through the trials that he went through, and thus none rose to the plinth that he rose to!

If we really believe that Prophet Muhammad could not have had any human frailties that you and I have, that he was not on an evolutionary journey, that he was not gaining by the minute; then how is Prophet Muhammad a role model for us to follow? The fact is that he pained and grieved, he experienced anxiety, at times he was shaken to the core; yet he overcame. The Quran says, "We know well that your chest is constricted by the things that they say." (15:97) He was experiencing human emotions, sentiments and the need for reassurance and he was growing through it all! Lady Ayesha asked the Prophet, "Why do you stand at night crying and beseeching Allah when He has said that He has forgiven you all your sins that have gone before and those that are to come?" The Prophet replied, "Indeed, He has! But should I not be a grateful slave to Allah?" As if he was saying I can't thank Him enough and I feel a sense of sinfulness that I can't thank Him adequately.

The Prophet went through the same journey that me and you are going through. If we deny this then he cannot be a role-model for us for he would be a superhuman. I do not need superhumans; they are not an example for me. I arise from the cradle of animality and try to attain to humanity, and from humanity I try to rise to the level of refined spirituality. I need a role-model who is on the same journey as I am! My state of poverty drives me to steal, cheat and lie. His state of poverty does not move him from his impeccable morality and virtues. My state of being alone and having excessive enemies drives me towards revenge. He was surrounded by his enemies at the conquest of Mecca, but his godly-compassion guided him to bestow freedom upon them. He experienced all the human emotions but he is able to do the right thing. That is the role-model that I want!

We believe that the Prophet had *'ilm al-ghayb,* the knowledge of the unseen of everything. Of course, he foretold future events accurately and he has given the signs of the end of time. However, what does God say about knowledge of the unseen? "Say, O Prophet: I do not say that God's treasures are with me, nor do I say that I know the things that are beyond the reach of human perception (the unseen), nor do I say that I am an angel. I but follow what is revealed to me." (6:50) Then God instructs, "Say, O Prophet: It is not within my power to bring benefit or avert harm from myself, except as God may please. And if I knew that which is beyond the reach of human perception (the unseen), surely, I would have received abundant good fortune and no evil would ever have touched me. I am nothing but a warner, and a giver of glad tidings unto people who will believe." (7:188)

He is saying look, if I knew the unseen, I would have reaped the benefits of the knowledge of the unseen and no evil would have befallen me. What was he trying to convey? What are these verses saying? When Allah decides that it is appropriate for the Prophet to have some relevant information of the unknown, only then does he receive it and only to the extent that He wants the Prophet to know. Of course the Prophet had that calibre where at will he could know many things beyond human reach however, it is Allah who has the decisive say. Allah wipes clean whatever He wants, and Allah establishes whatever He wants, and He has the Mother of the Book. If the Messenger of Allah were to have been endowed with the sort of knowledge of the unseen that we attribute to him, then he could not be a role model for anyone.

Listen to this with an open mind. We often hear that the eighth Imam knew that the date, which he was about to eat, had poison inside it but he ate it anyway. Really!? Compare this to what Imam Ali said on the night that he was struck with the fatal blow. Imam Ali was approached by Imam Hasan as he made his way to the mosque to lead the morning prayer. He was asked by his son, "Is it true that you have had a premonition that you are going to die?" Imam Ali replied, "I have had a dream and if it is true then I will be assassinated." Imam Hasan responds, "Then why are you going into the mosque!? Let me go and lead the prayers instead of you." Do you know what Imam Ali said next? "No soul knows what it shall earn tomorrow, and no soul knows in what land it shall die." (31:34) As if to say, "To the best of my knowledge, it may happen tonight but I don't have the decisive and final knowledge of God."

One of the reasons the Quran is insistent upon negating such godly attributes from the blessed Prophet is because otherwise the entire religion would become Prophet-centric and not God-centric, It is very unfortunate that today's Islam has become Prophet-centric and *ma'sūm*-centric. God has been removed altogether! That beautiful godliness, the direct connection with God – where is it? Where has it gone? We are the followers of Prophet Muhammad – the greatest monotheist. We are the followers of Ali ibn Abi Talib – another grand monotheist. Show me anywhere in the life of Imam Ali where he has not been totally God-centric. He was the closest one to Prophet Muhammad. There was no one who was nurtured by Prophet Muhammad as much as Imam Ali, but show me when he was Prophet-centric as opposed to God-centric. He was absolutely God-centric! There was nothing but God-centricity for him!

This is why the Quranic Revelation is repeatedly commanding Muhammad, the Messenger, to tell the people that he does not know the unseen so that they are not distracted from their goal. So, when God says, "Verily, in the Apostle of God you have the best example for anyone who wishes to attain God and the Last Day" it means that he must be studied. His life and conduct must be known by one and all. The orientalists are saying if only there was one more like Prophet Muhammad in the present day, he would bring peace and stability to the warring factions and nations of this world. They have studied his example! They see how he went beyond his own followers and brokered peace, created a league of nations, established human rights, and brought about God-centricity. When the women who are not Muslim study his example, they realise that he was the first to speak of women rights. He was the first one to give equality between women and men in their spiritual capacity.

People often criticise the initial orientalists for claiming that Prophet Muhammad's faith was spread by the sword. Empires that have spread by the sword have "crumbled with the sword", but Prophet Muhammad's message continues to grow. This man was something else! They say that Prophet Muhammad did not have the advantage that Jesus had of the "church" or speaking inside the cradle, and yet look at how he has established a God-centred faith in such a vast region. Look at how his precepts of justice, righteousness, and spirituality enabled the subsequent Muslim civilisation to flourish and proliferate. His example needs to be studied very closely with brutal honesty, sincerity, and truthfulness.

After reading many hadith that give the Prophet and the Imams super-human statuses, I have come to the conclusion that I am not going to rely on such hadith to appreciate Prophet Muhammad, Imam Ali, Imam Hasan, Imam Husayn, Imam Sadiq and the other blessed Imams. Instead I will study and look into their persons, and see what they were for myself. By God, this soul is humbled and in awe of the grand example of Prophet Muhammad and his blessed progeny! Every heart and mind will truly acknowledge that Muhammad and Ali were great. When we look at Imam Sadiq, we exclaim, "He dwarfs the intellectual giants like Plato and Aristotle." He was way ahead of his time. Therefore, their examples need to be studied. However, we must remove them from "the level of God" that we attribute to them, advertently or inadvertently. We need to understand them as human beings and be brutally honest when we study them.

Study the Quran. You will see that Prophet Muhammad, like his grandfather prophet Ibrahim, is taking a beautiful journey. The only difference is that we do not find Prophet Muhammad faltering. It is phenomenal! However, the Quran will give you insight about Prophet Muhammad's humanness. Initially, when the Sūra were being revealed the Prophet feared that he may forget parts and so he recited the verses quickly so that they could be recorded and memorised by his companions. Now, you may find this strange. You might be thinking, how is it possible that somebody like the Prophet could fear that he might forget? But this attitude is due to our assumption that the Prophet could never forget. Check this assumption with the Qur̲an. You will see so clearly that in the middle of Sūra al-Qiyāma, whilst it was being revealed, there is suddenly a pause and God reassures the Prophet. He says, "Do not move your tongue in haste, it is on Us to ensure that it is gathered and it will be for Us to make its meaning clear." (75:16-19)

At times, our understanding of the Prophet is marked by our own assumptions as opposed to looking at history and understanding the Prophet for what he was worth and recognising his "humanness". Look at his interactions with his wives. When his jealous wives complained he felt sorry for them and said he would not repeat what hurt them because of this human aspect that he had. In response to this appeasement God said, "Why are you making prohibited what Allah has made permissible for you?" But he was displaying the beauty of his humanity in wanting to keep his wives happy by conceding to them and not disappointing them even though their demands were unreasonable. Similarly, recall the incident when Lady Ayesha went missing, and the people started to make accusations against her. The blessed Prophet was distressed at the constant gossip. His being distressed demonstrates his humanness. Of course, the Quran later exonerated her of any form of misconduct, thereby putting the matter to rest.

Another instance where we become aware of the Prophet's humanness is when God says to the faithful, "When you are invited to the Prophet's house for food, eat and go. Do not spend too much time. This troubles the Prophet and he feels embarrassed to tell you this, but God does not feel embarrassment."

(33:53) Why did the Prophet feel embarrassed? It is due to his humanness that he feels hesitant because he does not want to be disrespectful. Look at his humanness! This is the point we are trying to make. The Prophet needs to be studied in his human capacity. The Quran says, "Say, O Prophet: I am but a mortal man like all of you." (18:110) And, then again it repeats the same thing, "Say, O Prophet: I am but a mortal man like all of you." (41:6) The Quran narrates that the Prophet was being asked to bring a variety of miracles such as causing springs to flow from the ground, producing gardens of palm trees and dates, causing the heavens to fall to the earth in pieces or having a house of gold and to ascend to the sky and bring back a book. The Quran commands the Prophet to respond by saying, "Glory be to Allah! Am I but a mortal Messenger?" (17:90-93) As if to say these things are beyond my reach and outside my capacity, I am but a mortal. Muhammad, the Messenger of God, is the one who in his humanness has arrived at a state that is so supreme that God makes him an example for all mankind. That is the beauty and the charm of Prophet Muhammad – that as a human being, with all the human traits, he arrived at this height of existence.

Now, look at the deliberations of Allamah Tabatabai on this verse, "And if you are in doubt as to that which We have revealed to Our servant, then produce a chapter from his like and call on your witnesses besides Allah if you are truthful." (2:23) Allamah Tabatabai says the meaning of "his like" is the likes of Prophet Muhammad – that is one who has never read or written. This verse is challenging the Meccans to find somebody like him, and then ask that individual to produce something as magnificent as this Quran. Bear in mind that the majority of the Arabs at that time could not read or write.

One of the *dua* attributed to him was, "O Lord! Show me things as they really are" Another was, "O Lord! Increase me in knowledge!" Allow me to see the secrets of what You have created – secrets upon secrets – and baffle this mind even further!

The Quran states that if any of these prophets say be devoted to me apart from Allah, they will burn in the pits of hell! By implication, this shows that the prophets are what they are and, become what they become in their "human" capacity. When someone in their human capacity can arrive at that pedestal - *Subḥānallah* That is the greatest miracle! Imagine, a mere mortal can arrive at this level of existence.

Again in Sūra al-Nisā, we see the Prophet operating in his human capacity. A case was brought to the Prophet where it was claimed that some Jewish people had stolen, and the Prophet adjudicated against them based on the weight of the evidence. In fact, what had happened was that it was some of the Muslims who had stolen a certain item and then planted it in the Jewish household. After this judgment, God revealed the treachery to the Prophet, "O Prophet, they are trying to misguide you, and had it not been the favour of God, they would have indeed succeeded." (4:112-113)

So, the Prophet reopened the case in light of the new evidence and re-issued his verdict. Again, this demonstrates his humanness and shows that he could be deceived just as we can. Again, verses describe enemies of God coming to the Prophet and deceiving him of their faith, "And of the people is he whose speech pleases you in worldly life, and he calls Allah to witness as to what is in his heart, yet he is the fiercest of opponents." (2:204) His humanness is exactly why he is the perfect role model.

You cannot be a role model if you do not operate in your human capacity. Now, imagine if after being totally human, you arrive at that rank of impeccability where you do not go against God in the slightest because you are so conscious of Him. That is an example for mankind, and that is what Prophet Muhammad was. He arrived at that rank. Imagine being an orphan, a poor man surrounded by enemies – yet his morals are unaffected! We all know that he gave rights to the those who were not Muslim, but he goes far beyond that. He spoke of the rights of animals and ordained that they be treated with compassion. Somebody had brandished an animal upon the nose and the Prophet stated that this individual would be raised in hell for inflicting upon an animal. Look at how phenomenal this man was.

He is born in a warring and barbaric culture, yet look at how refined he is as an upright and moral individual. All of these factors that would have caused others in his position to fall and yet through them arose the finest human that has ever walked on the face of this earth. He was somebody that Gabriel saluted. Imagine how grand this Prophet is. When we study the Prophet, we truly realise his spiritual grandeur, universal compassion, godly virtues, sublime wisdom and intellect, political dexterity and societal pragmatism. He is remarkable! He is the only man who can assure the success of the individual, the Muslim community, and humanity at large.

Let us be enlightened about our Prophet. What did he do? How did he lead his life? What did he stand for? The problem is we have so many naïve assumptions We do not believe that the he felt the human pain that me and you feel. We feel that he was assisted by miracles and that he was informed of all events that were to transpire. We assume him to have been endowed with superhuman powers, like certain mythical figures or the Hindu avatars of god. These things cannot be true. In fact, they cancel out his great achievement as a mere mortal, which is a great disservice to him. Moreover, such claims run counter to the Quranic description of him and ultimately mean that he cannot be an example for us. The fact is that he was a human; people gained confidence through the fact that he was human. He did pain. His eyes watered and he cried at the death of his son. It is narrated that he said, "O child, your death brings pain that is unbearable, but this tongue shall not utter anything that is displeasing to my Lord." How beautiful is this statement?

When the Prophet was dying, lady Fatimah uttered a poem in midst of her sorrow, which was attributed to the Prophet's uncle the great Abu Talib. "O you who is the cause for the skies to bestow plentifully upon the earth. O the one who is a refuge for the orphan and the widows. What shall we do after you?" The Prophet replied, "Fatima, do not utter these verses. Utter this verse instead, 'Muhammad is nothing but a messenger. Before him, many messengers have gone. So, if he dies or is killed, shall you turn away from your faith?" (3:144) Imagine, how impeccable and God-conscious he was even during the pangs of death.

Look at the humility of this man. He would sit on the earth milking a goat and he would ride on a mule, in spite of being the leader of all in Medina. Where do you find a person like him? When Imam Ali was questioned, "How do you eat such stale bread, which we cannot even break? How do you bite into it?" Imam Ali replied with tears in his eyes, "This food would have been amply sufficed as the feast of Eid for the Messenger of God." Do you know that he would tie rocks upon his belly so that the pangs of hunger would not kill him? He did not allow himself to eat whilst any member of his Ummah remained hungry. He was like a caring father and mother for the faithful.

Once Gabriel offered him the keys of the treasures of the heavens and the earth He responded, "Gabriel take them back. The day in which He feeds me, I will thank Him, and the day in which He keeps me hungry, I shall persevere." As if the Prophet was saying I do not want to think that I have any control over my own affairs. I want to be fully reliant upon my God. The world has never seen anybody like Muhammad the Prophet. He is the only one whose example can liberate us of the intellectual shackles that we have imposed on our minds, the moral restrictions that make us less than humans, and spiritual depravity within us. He was nothing but the light of God in its entirety. He arrived at that level of fine existence.

I often say that the conduct of Prophet Muhammad that the Muslims have understood is only things like how he ate, how he sat, and other outer functions. But nobody looks deeper to understand how he was in himself. His real conduct was that he left everything to God, he always made sure that he did the right thing, and, he was extremely humble in front of God – sincere, and absolutely surrendered. When he faced the enemy in battle, do you know what he would say sometimes? He would say that everybody feels fear and he would recite there is no ability nor power save with Allah after which he would proceed. Imam Ali says that when the battle would reach its peak and the fear would grip us, we would stand behind the Prophet for no one was more forceful in breaking the ranks of the disbelievers than the Prophet.

Even in the midst of the battle the Prophet was so just and Godly. The orientalists state that he was the one who introduced discipline within the ranks of such undisciplined waring people that even within the battlefield the Muslims would abandon fighting and attend to prayers in rows behind the Prophet. In the battle of Badr, the Meccans lost and fled the battlefield abandoning their dead, such was the fear in their hearts. The Prophet instructed his companions to bury the bodies of the deceased Meccans. They reacted, "O Prophet, but these are the enemies of Allah and His Messenger!" He replied, "They are human beings and so deserve a dignified burial." This was the blessed Prophet! Before the battle would commence, he would give these instructions to his followers, "Do not chase fleeing soldiers. If somebody should fall from their stead, do not put them to death. Do not burn trees nor uproot any plants. Do not burn their houses. Do not kill their women. Do not transgress against their children. Do not mutilate a dead body." Imagine, he was a person of such moral standing in the midst of such barbarians and their barbaric cultures and customs.

We see that his conduct, in the sense of his real conduct, is missing from the community altogether. If his real conduct was being emulated, then the community would not be where it is. I am talking about our Muslim community – the way in which we kill each other. Allah states, "Verily, as for those who have broken the unity of their faith and have become sects – you (O Muhammad) have *nothing* to do with them. Behold, their case rests with God and in time He will make them understand what they were doing." (6:159) Aren't these verses saying something to us? Instead of killing ourselves like this, we should be following the *real* Prophet and the *real* Quran, so that we arrive at that glorious state of wanting the best for the whole of humanity. Was the blessed Prophet not the one who established an Ummah withstanding variety of religious persuasions and allowed each group religious freedom and enactment of their own law systems? It is only after we follow this noble example that the magnificent one, the Mahdi will come to lead us a right to the utmost success.

The real being of the Prophet was that humble man who was so completely surrendered to God that at every point there was he and his God. Whenever he suffered loss, what we learn from his conduct is that he achieved an inner state of submission and contentment with the decree of God whereby he stated, "O Allah, it was Yours by priority, it has come back to You." When he faced uncertainty, he did not become overly dismayed or distressed, instead he was able to let go and say, "I place my trust in Allah." If anybody would annoy him, he would immediately compose himself and smile back. His wives have said that, "At times, we would say and do things that angered him. The colour of his face would change however, he was never unjust to us. He merely stopped talking with us until we detracted." This was his conduct – an extremely gentle conduct. He would always forgive his enemy. In fact, his behaviour towards everyone he came across was reminiscent of the parent, in terms of how a parent always cares for his children and makes excuses for his children.

It is very sad and unfortunate that his followers on both sides, Sunni and Shia, have forgotten him. He does not have an integral place in our Islam anymore. He has become a cosmetic part of Islam. The majority of the Muslims assume that he was the greatest Prophet by virtue of attributing superhuman nobility and miraculous tendencies to him, which they have either heard from the pulpits or been taught in the madrasa. This has resulted in our current situation where he has become untouchable and unreachable and he cannot possibly be emulated or followed! What makes the situation more tragic is that the Word of God, the Quran, indicates his humanness very clearly and teaches us his exemplary conduct; however, no one in the community reads the Quran. If you are disturbed by all of what has been said, then pick up the Quran and read about Prophet Muhammad. Try to understand how profound this man was in his humanness, instead of merely assuming. Then study him thoroughly. Consider the reforms he brought, his world-view that drove him to unite the people and create a pluralistic state in Medina. Consider his understanding and treatment of the other, the non-Muslim. Nothing can serve the Muslim community more than a very close examination of the life and conduct of the blessed Prophet.

We find this narration about the Prophet, and it depicts the way he loved. It is said that Imam Husayn was finding it difficult to speak — he began to speak a little late in life. So, on an occasion the Prophet was either commencing prayers or cajoling the young Imam to speak. The Prophet said, *Allāhu akbar* (God is great) and Imam Husayn replied, *Allāhu akbar*. So the Prophet quickly said, *Allāhu akbar* again and Imam Husayn responded with, *Allāhu akbar* again. The Prophet repeated *Allāhu akbar* seven times because he was rejoicing that Imam Husayn was beginning to speak. Imagine, like any human being Prophet Muhammad was so overcome with joy when he witnessed his grandson beginning to speak that he said seven *takbīr*. In fact, prompted by this event, it is speculated that the blessed Prophet introduced supererogatory *takbīr* in the daily prayers.

Night Ten

We said yesterday that the Prophet's life needs to be studied and it is of the utmost importance that we study it critically. The Prophet needs to be seen as a human being, that is in his human context, in order for him to be a role model so that we can emulate his example. He needs to be studied in terms of the different aspects of his life: Muhammad as an individual, Muhammad as *rasūl Allah*, Muhammad as the family man, Muhammad as the statesman, Muhammad as the friend, Muhammad as the helper of the poor and orphans, Muhammad in Mecca, Muhammad in Medina, Muhammad in the battlefield, Muhammad at the conquest of Mecca, and Muhammad at the body of Hamza and so on. When studying all these aspects, we need to be mindful of the contexts of the different aspects in order for them to yield meaningfully. This will ensure that he can be emulated as the human model that will lead us towards a Godly life.

The Prophet of God is a prime example for the one who wants to meet with Allah – for the one who is desirous of Allah. "Being desirous of Allah" means becoming Godly, Godlike or God-centric. In the process of attaining this purpose of becoming Godly, the Prophet Muhammad is an integral part. Therefore he needs to be studied very closely and carefully, putting all of our assumptions to one side, so that we are able to uncover the real Muhammad. When we study Prophet Muhammad in the works of the scholars, who have done a brilliant job, we realise that their pre-existing beliefs and assumptions have blurred their understanding of Prophet Muhammad altogether. Sometimes it is better to look at Prophet Muhammad through the eyes of the Orientalists because they have no attachment or emotional investment with the Prophet of Allah. Therefore, they are more likely to look at him objectively. Sometimes they may offend but if we are searching for the truth, then we will not get offended because we will be able to discern truth from falsity.

During your critical and sincere study of the different facets of Prophet Muhammad, you will inevitably come across a few issues that are inconsistent. For instance, the Quran commands the Prophet to say, "Tell them: I do not know the unseen", but he made several prophecies, which were all accurate. Now, try to reconcile properly without having the biases in our minds. The reason for the Quran expressing this is that Prophet Muhammad cannot, and would not, be given knowledge of everything for otherwise there would be no challenge for him. And in fact, this is the case for all prophets, Imams and saints. You and I are challenged on the basis of not knowing or having uncertainty. At times, the Prophet's heart was gripped with uncertainty, yet observe how he behaved in such circumstances – how he overcame it through total reliance upon Allah. This is the charm of the prophetic example. He does not know what will happen to him and yet he was virtuous and upright. This constitutes the most valid role model. We can emulate a person who suffers like us and has uncertainty of tomorrow like us, and yet he still manages to do the right thing.

Therefore, the relevance of Prophet Muhammad, as the prime example, is that he is integral to us fulfilling our whole purpose. Let us briefly recap what we said with regards to the purpose of humanity. The first purpose we said is that we become intellectually liberated and begin to fulfil ourselves intellectually and grow. The second purpose is that we become morally refined, which incidentally is being witnessed in humanity as a whole. In fact, we must contribute to the discourse on human values that are befitting for one and all regardless of colour, denomination, status or gender. These universal values yield "the human rights" that befit humanity as humanity, regardless of whether we are Christians, Hindus, Jews, theists or atheists. The third purpose is that inherent yearning for a deep sense of existence.

Despite becoming morally refined and intellectually fulfilled, we are not satisfied. There is a deep-seated need inside me to be rooted in an existence where I can actually say that I am living. That level of yearning calls for a substantive life, whereby substantively I am arriving at something. It is a seed that sprouts, becomes a tree, and bears fruit. This is what me and you want. We want that deep-seated meaning! We want to find God, for it is only through God that we can arrive at a purposeful existence. Otherwise our existence seems to be superficial and arbitrary. The Quran explains that those who live such an arbitrary and superficial life, it is as if whatever they have achieved in this life is like dust seated on a rock; as soon as they turn to retrieve it, a gust of wind blows it away because there is no rooting in that soul. It is at this level that we need to find God.

So today we are discussing Imamah. As we go into this discussion, we will show that the blessed Imam Ali ibn Abi Talib was not imposed as a leader upon the community. He could never be imposed. You cannot impose a leader upon the people. Imagine, if the Prophet went to Mecca and said to the people, "I am the Prophet, and you need to follow me." The Meccans would never have followed him. Only after they were convinced of his claim did they hand over the reins of authority to Prophet Muhammad. Only then will his "model example" be accepted and impactful. It is like me saying to you, "Allah has sent me to rule over you." What would be your response? You will say, "Dream on!" Authority has to be willingly given by the people for it to be effective especially divine authority.

The blessed Prophet convinced the people with the intellectual and moral content of the message from God. Thus, they handed over the reins of their destiny and lives to Prophet Muhammad, and that is why he was so effective in governing them. You cannot impose a divine leader upon the people – this is something that is quite obvious. So what did Prophet Muhammad do? He was extremely mindful of this. Thus, within the pseudo-democratic-type of mechanics that existed within his context, in which he had certain rights as the leader, he took the initiative of designating the most qualified person as his successor to lead the Ummah, which was the blessed Ali ibn Abi Talib.

In the sermon at *Ghadīr*, he said, "Do I not enjoy priority over your souls more than you yourselves?" Then he recited the verse, "Allah and His Prophet have priority over the faithful than they do over themselves." The people present responded, "Indeed you do, O Messenger of God! You do have that priority over us." Then he stated, "If that is the case then Ali is your *mawlā* (master) after this day." So the Prophet definitely did not impose Imam Ali onto the people, otherwise his example as a divine guide becomes redundant.

So, the Prophet initially confirmed whether the people accepted his own right over themselves, and only after their agreement did he state his preference that Ali be their leader after him. But the question for us is: in what capacity was Imam Ali appointed? Obviously, it was as the best, most qualified, person to drive the community towards its purpose. What was the purpose? Intellectual liberation, moral refinement and acquisition of God-centricity – to become God-like! That is the reason why the blessed Ali ibn Abi Talib was the only choice.

I ask my Shia brothers that if somebody has decided to truly follow and emulate Imam Ali ibn Abi Talib, what difference does it make whether that individual calls him the first Imam or the fourth Caliph? The people who are concerned over whether he is the first Imam or fourth Caliph are equally not following him.

His example is redundant for both. Think about it carefully. Both sides have reduced Ali as a means to argue over mere labels! The Sunni have this hadith that the Prophet said, "O Ali, your example is like the Ka'ba. You do not need to go out to the people. The people will come running and converge to you." The Prophet said, "Me and Ali are the two fathers of the Ummah." Ali is the father of the Ummah, whether you are Shia or Sunni, or whatever you are. Remember, the Ummah of Prophet Muhammad did not only have Muslims within it. Rather, it comprised of Jews, Muslims and pagans. Therefore, Ali is the father of humanity after the Prophet.

In history, there is the event at *saqīfah* in which there was a struggle and you know the history better than I. The Caliph at that time, Abu Bakr, appointed Caliph Umar, after which Caliph Umar created a council that appointed Caliph Uthman. After Caliph Uthman's caliphate, the Ummah unanimously converged and asked the blessed Imam Ali ibn Abi Talib to become the Caliph. So, whereas the others were only appointed by an individual or small group, Imam Ali was appointed by the whole Ummah. Everyone recognised his Godly character and deemed him the best suited to lead them.

Look at our community. The fact that we can swear and curse at each other and cannot tolerate our differences or plurality shows that we have moved away from the example of the *wilāya* of Imam Ali. Hence, I ask the Shias fine he is the "first" Imam, now if the 1.7 billion Muslims were to agree that he is the first Imam, will you then be better human beings after that? It is the same situation and attitudes that the prophets faced – we have not changed at all. We only want people to give lip service that Ali was the first Imam. What difference will that make? If they insist that he is the fourth Caliph and we are stuck repeating that he is the first Imam, then both the groups have equally not understood this man. His greatness and example transcend the labels that are so important to us.

I said yesterday that I have become a little disenchanted with the reliance on hadith in order to understand our role models because of how they exaggerate and attribute superhuman status to the Prophet and Imams. We need to examine a person for what he is worth beyond the hadith literature. By Allah, when we truly see this man, Ali ibn Abi Talib, we stand bewildered! After Prophet Muhammad, I would definitely conclude that there was no man upon the earth greater than the blessed Ali ibn Abi Talib. It is only because we know the example of Prophet Muhammad that Imam Ali is dwarfed and put into perspective. This is how profound he is!

I will give an example of one of the principles he abided by – his principle of righteousness and justice. There is this notion that the ends justify the means. He did not agree with this at all. He stated that if the means are not righteous, then it is unrighteous to justify them. When he became the Caliph, he was advised not to remove the governors that the previous Caliphs had instated as it would be politically unsound and imprudent. His response was, "It is true that I should keep them in their positions in order to secure my power, but they have been so corrupt and unjust that my sense of righteousness will not allow me to keep them in such public positions." Think about this – is it not amazing?

When Abu Bakr became the Caliph, we are told, Abu Sufyan approached Imam Ali saying, "We have kinship so take assistance from us to retrieve your right from the son of Abu Quhafah." Imam Ali replied, "I will not take the aid of falsehood to combat falsehood." Think about this, this is God-centricity in its entirety. During the battle of Siffin, Muawiya's forces had taken control of the river bank and subsequently decided to cut-off the water supply to Imam Ali's forces. The battalions of Malik al-Ashtar and Imam Hasan were sent to retrieve control of the river bank, which they did. Malik al-Ashtar passed a message to Imam Ali, "Let us withhold access to the river and they will submit." In response, Imam Ali rode up to the river, cupped water in his hand and gave an eloquent sermon in which he said to his enemies, "O people, the Jews and Christians drink from this water. Animals drink from this water. Come and partake in this wholesome sustenance that Allah has prepared for you." He did not withhold water from his enemies. Notice, how he was abiding by the principle that the ends do not justify corrupt means. This is only one example of many that I could give. Where do you find such a person?

The *wilāya* of the Imams has been totally misunderstood – in fact, it has not been understood at all. These beautiful Imams were as "human" as their grandfather. The blessed Imam Ali was asked by his enemy during the peak of battle, "Who are you, O magnanimous man?" He replied, "I am a lowly slave from amongst the many slaves of Muhammad." When Lady Zaynab told her nephew, Imam Ali Ibn Husayn, "O child, you will kill yourself with this excessive devotion to God" and he did not listen, she spoke to Jabir ibn Abd Allah Ansari. "Tell him not to stand for whole nights in devotion and fast so excessively." When Jabir conveyed this, the Imam replied, "What is my worship in comparison to the worship of my grandfathers: the Messenger of Allah and Imam Ali?" These people were of the prophetic substance, but they were totally "human". They were not beyond human. Hence, their example in *wilāya* is relevant, otherwise it is redundant. Their *wilāya*, after Prophet Muhammad, is to lead people to that state of intellectual liberation, moral refinement, and God-centricity in every moment. Their true teaching is not jurisprudence; it is not how to wash your arms! Their true teaching is about the *waḥdāniya*, the Oneness, and *aḥadiya*, the uniqueness, of Allah. Their true teaching is how to arrive at that deep sense of spirituality.

We have a narration, "The first, the middle and the final: all of us are Muhammad." The naïve Shia community thinks that this narration implies that all twelve Imams are of a single personality and would act in exactly the same manner in any given situation. Such fanciful beliefs make no sense at all. They were all unique individuals; they were all very different. We stated in a previous lecture that even the prophets were very different. One was *kalīm*; the other was *khalīl*; another was *ṣafī*; and another was *rūḥ*. Regarding these prophets, Allah has said the following two statements in the Quran, "We do not distinguish between any of them," (2:285) and, "We have given preference to some over others." (2:253) Now, will anybody deny that Ali ibn Abi Talib was better than the rest of the Imams? Will anybody deny that Hasan and Husayn were better than any of the other nine Imams? Will anybody deny that the twelfth Imam is better than the ones that precede him apart from Imams Hasan and Husayn? No. There was distinction between them – they were all different people. They had different sentiments. They all faced challenges differently.

There is no guarantee that two Imams would do the same thing in any given situation. We know for a fact that Imam Hasan and Husayn were very different. Imam Hasan was very contained whereas Imam Husayn was very passionate. On occasions, Imam Husayn would say to Imam Hasan, "Let us not withstand this from Muawiya!" Imam Hasan would reply, "No, we will tolerate it." On an occasion, Imam Husayn said to Imam Hasan, "Pass me the sword and allow me to strike Abdul Rahman in order to relieve my heart of this rage and this grief." Imam Hasan struck ibn Muljim and then passed the sword to his brother.

All the Imams were very different but all offered accurate responses. It is not possible to predict whether two Imams would have acted similarly in any given situation. However, you can be assured that they would both have acted righteously. In fact, there are always multiple responses that one could give in any situation that would qualify as "righteous". There is rarely only one response. So, there was this natural plurality that existed between the different Imams – a beautiful individuality to all of them.

Now, our Sunni brothers are beginning to admit that the

Imams and Lady Fatima were a rank above the rest. Undoubtedly, the wives of the Prophet are most definitely part of the blessed Prophet's *ahl al-bayt*. However, by priority a person's *ahl al-bayt* are his children – his blood. They constitute the first tier of one's *ahl al-bayt* because one can divorce a wife; however, in the case of a child one would have to dis-own him or her. There is a huge distinction between the two. Now, the Shia have to admit that a wife is also among one's *ahl al-bayt* – the second tier – and this is quite obvious. The Sunni also have to admit that the blood relation of a man are one's "real" household because they cannot be transient. Thus, Lady Fatima, her husband and their children constitute the blessed Prophet's *ahl al-bayt*.

Therefore, *rijs* – meaning impurities – were specifically kept away from *these* particular individuals by Divine Will, which included the impurity of worshipping other than God, disbelief, hypocrisy, lying, greed, jealousy among other spiritual and moral defects. Therefore, their hearts were like their grandfather; they were beautiful souls that were totally reliant on God. We find in the narrations of both these sects that only Imam Ali ibn Abi Talib, Lady Fatima, Hasan and Husayn accompanied the Prophet to the *mubāhala* with the Christians. Thus, we must admit, regardless of our sectarian belonging, that the spiritual rank of these people was far greater than any of the companions or wives of the Prophet. The Quran commands, "Say: I do not ask anything but deep-seated affection with my near ones." (42:23)

Now, what does their *wilāya* constitute? There are two levels at which we need to discuss this. We stated that God-centricity is the absolute purpose, and that in this life we are attaining salvation and success through God-centricity. The message of God-centricity was always accompanied by prophets who were integral not only in demonstrating a God-centric life, but also in fulfilling the human need for exemplars that could be trusted, loved and related to. There is a deep-seated need in every soul to associate with, and relate to somebody. Thus, we always have and need relationships. The most natural relationship that we form is with our parents. Imam Sadiq has said that when you promise your children anything, you must fulfil your promise because they see you as their gods. It is a natural state that the human soul needs another figure that they can understand, relate to, and deeply love. In fact, that deep degree of love becomes transformative – it reforms us.

Can you deny that crying for our beloved Imam Husayn ibn Ali purges the heart of its impurities? It does – it is a fact! When a greedy or an unforgiving person is made to shed tears for the Imam, they will be able to leave their money or forgive with ease. An insecure person becomes secure and empowered in the love of Husayn ibn Ali. Who can deny this? Therefore, the *wilāya* of the Imams is to have this beautiful belonging with Prophet Muhammad and the household of Prophet Muhammad, a parental love and bonding so that we can rely upon their examples. Love their examples and know that their examples will give us success in terms attaining our purpose.

The other meaning of *wilāya* is that we learn from the Prophet and Imams. Look at their knowledge base. For instance, the accuracy with which Imam Sadiq spoke about cosmology – how he has described the universe, which actually coincides with what current astrophysicists and other theorists are saying about the cosmos. You will exclaim, "How is it possible that this man was so accurate!?" Ibn Arabi got cosmology wrong. May God have mercy on him and bless him abundantly for he was a great saint, in which there is no denying. He possibly borrowed from Aristotelian cosmology; hence, he talks about the celestial figures similar to that of Aristotle.

Imam Sadiq spoke of the "expanding universe" and "constant motion" as the absolute property of the physical existence of the universe. He talked about multiple realms of existence. How can this man, one thousand four hundred years ago, be so inconsistent with the Greek astronomers and philosophers of his time who were contributing to this area of knowledge, and state something so different to what was understood of the cosmos back then and yet be so accurate in terms of what he said? How could he have said that which has only been verified by current cosmology less than 60 years ago? Look at the knowledge base, he has insights on marine life, plants, oceans, ecology, and more.

Imam Sadiq also spoke about the Sharia in ways that would be considered to be the reformation of the Sharia. He emphasised the necessity of doing one Eid. He also vehemently opposed all sectarianism. Thus, he insisted that his followers must pray with the "other", visit the "other", and have good familial relations with the "other". In fact, this was the attitude from the sixth Imam all the way to the eleventh Imam, all of them spoke in the same manner. How has the Shia community gone so wrong? I say to you O Shias, you want to die for the Imams, first start following them! Follow them first then you won't have to kill yourselves. Their example will give life to you all. The Imams are the givers of life.

Look at the way in which they were reforming the Sharia law. Imam Sadiq, with regards to the animals slaughtered during the pilgrimage said, "Take the meat out of Mina." The people reacted, "But your grandfathers used to insist that it should remain in Mina." He explained, "There are now so many more pilgrims in Mina, which has resulted in quantities of meat that the people in Mina cannot possibly consume. Therefore, take it outside of Mina and feed the poor." Look at this man. Look at how enlightened his thinking was. Instead of allowing meat to be wasted in Mina because that it what the Sharia was perceived to be, he showed us that the true essence was something else. Therefore, we can add here that *wilāya* also means to adapt the Sharia in accordance with the circumstances, or the context, so that the optimal level of God-centricity is maintained.

Look at the way these Imams were. Their "real" example has truly been abandoned by the community – by both communities. If you study their examples in different aspects of life, you see that they were absolutely virtuous and moral. They would never compromise their principles of righteousness and justice. However, by far the greatest contribution of these Imams was their teachings on the Unity of God. Read their teachings! The teachings of every Imam are beautiful. For instance, Imam Ali says of God, "He is with everything, and yet He does not touch anything. He is other than everything, and yet there is no distance between Him and anything."

In another sermon, Imam Ali says, "He shall never come to an end, and He has always been as He is. There is nothing like Him! He, First and Foremost, is a Unique Lord in His Exaltation, able through His Might, holy through His Sublimity, and proud of His Majesty! No vision can realize Him, nor can anyone ever see Him. He is strong, invincible, seeing, hearing, clement, wise, affectionate and kind. One who attempts to describe Him can never do so, and one who attempts to describe His attributes can never do so. His blessing reaches those who get to know Him. He is near and yet He is far. He is far and yet He is near." How beautiful is that?

One of the later Imams has said, "O You the One who is in every direction that I look towards." How beautifully the Imams announce the Unity of God. The only purpose for their sublime phrases was to direct the minds and hearts of their listeners and readers towards God-centricity. Their examples need to be studied very carefully. Read Dua Kumayl where Imam Ali is talking to God in a variety of ways. The Prophet did say that, "My brother Ali has been gifted with eloquency." At one point he talks to God as a slave talks to a master. Then, after some paragraphs, Imam Ali talks to God as a person who has made a pact with another. And then he talks to God as if one is talking to the closest friend one has. He portrays the sentiments, "O Lord! I will burn in the flames. What is hurting is that I was crying and You turned a deaf ear to me. You saw me and You ignored me. I don't care if the rest of the world has abandoned me or not, but what is hurting me is what You have done!" How can anyone talk so openly with God? And then he says to God, "I have invested everything in You, O Lord. I have given everything of mine to You. I have divorced the world. Now, I don't have anything but You. O Lord, shall You abandon me!?"

And then Imam Ali goes to another level, and talks to God in the way one talks to a mother. You know mothers – may God bless them for they are a reflection of God, and if they are gone then go their graves, talk to them and pray to God for them. When we go to our mothers and sometimes offend them so much that they are silent and they turn their faces away, what do we say? O Mother, slap me. Swear at me. Shout at me. Curse me. Do anything and acknowledge me! O Mother, even in your slap, there is acknowledgement. Even in your shouting, at least there is the admission that I am yours! Imam Ali goes to that depth with Allah. He says, "O Lord, even if I were to bear your hell, how could I bear your separation?" Look at the way they are teaching us. Look at the *dua* of Imam Ali Ibn Husayn; look at how phenomenal they are. By the way, I am talking about the authentic *dua*, not the *dua* that we read in the name of the Imams. Look at Dua 'Arafah of Husayn ibn Ali, the sense of spirituality of Husayn ibn Ali.

Before concluding these talks, I want to leave you with one more important point. The prophets and Imams are human beings and their role is only to lead us to God. We associate intimately with the Prophet and his family because it is a deep-seated need within us, the need to form that bond and attachment with a symbol. They are the symbols. Musa, Isa, Ibrahim, Nuh, etc. – fall in love with all of them. Stand and say bless Adam, bless Nuh, Khidr, Musa, Isa, Dawud, Ibrahim, Muhammad , Ali, Hasan, Husayn, and lady Zahra. Bless all of them. Form this beautiful attachment with them However, their attachment is not to remove us from the centrality of God. The Quran is absolutely clear on this: centrality is for God alone! Prophet Muhammad, Imam Ali, prophets and angels all fall within a scheme of that centrality, so long as that attachment assists in becoming God-like.

As long as they assist in finding the blinding and burning passion and love of Allah, then it is all fine. But, if it moves us away from the love of God, then something has gone wrong. When the Imams acquire the position of God in our devotions or in the mosques, then something has gone terribly wrong. There has to be absolute God-centricity because the blessed Prophet Muhammad and beloved Imam Ali have taught us God-centricity. We do not love our mothers to the extent that it impedes us in our progression with Allah. Therefore, if you see the love of our beloved Prophet Muhammad and his blessed progeny in your hearts, know that it is a glimpse calling you towards the love of God. That is the end purpose, and that is the absolute! It is only in God's name that we fall in love with these beautiful divine servants of God.

Always remember that they are human. They had the same tests that every human being must go through. They weighed up situations as we do. They made decisions as we do. The difference is that they made decisions on the principles of righteousness and without any corruption from within their hearts. That is their noble example. Learn *tawḥīd* from them and learn to find that deep-seated spiritual connection through them. Thus, their example has the potential to lead us to God for they are Godly beings. And none more so than Husayn ibn Ali. I know for a fact that both God and His Messenger will forgive a soul that is immersed in the love of Husayn to the level that they find Husayn overpowering them – this is true! The way in which he was. His sense of spiritually is enough to cause any soul to lose its own senses!

www.ingramcontent.com/pod-product-compliance
Lightning Source LLC
Chambersburg PA
CBHW030524080526
44586CB00011B/318